Spain, 1

JOCELYN HUNT

 Routledge
Taylor & Francis Group

LONDON AND NEW YORK

First published 2001
by Routledge
2 Park Square, Milton Park, Abingdon, Oxon OX14 4RN

Simultaneously published in the USA and Canada
by Routledge
711 Third Avenue, New York, NY 10017

Routledge is an imprint of the Taylor & Francis Group, an informa business

© 2001 Jocelyn Hunt

Typeset in Akzidenz Grotesque and Perpetua by
Keystroke, Jacaranda Lodge, Wolverhampton

British Library Cataloguing in Publication Data
A catalogue record for this book is available from the British Library

Library of Congress Cataloging in Publication Data
Hunt, Jocelyn.
    Spain, 1474–1598 / Jocelyn Hunt.
       p. cm. – (Questions and analysis in history)
    Includes bibliographical references and index.
    1. Spain–History–Ferdinand and Isabella, 1479–1516. 2. Spain–
History–Charles I, 1516–1556. 3. Spain–History–Philip II, 1556–1598.
I. Title. II. Series.
DP162 .H86 2000
946–dc21   00-028187

ISBN 978-0-415-22266-2

CONTENTS

ILLUSTRATIONS

PLATES

MAPS

SERIES PREFACE

Most history textbooks now aim to provide the student with interpretation, and many also cover the historiography of a topic. Some include a selection of sources.

So far, however, there have been few attempts to combine *all* the skills needed by the history student. Interpretation is usually found within an overall narrative framework and it is often difficult to separate the two for essay purposes. Where sources are included, there is rarely any guidance as to how to answer the questions on them.

The Questions and Analysis series is therefore based on the belief that another approach should be added to those which already exist. It has two main aims.

The first is to separate narrative from interpretation so that the latter is no longer diluted by the former. Most chapters start with a background narrative section containing essential information. This material is then used in a section focusing on analysis through a specific question. The main purpose of this is to help to tighten up essay technique.

The second aim is to provide a comprehensive range of sources for each of the issues covered. The questions are of the type which appear on examination papers, and some have worked answers to demonstrate the techniques required.

The chapters may be approached in different ways. The background narratives can be read first to provide an overall perspective, followed by the analyses and then the sources. The alternative method is to work through all the components of each chapter before going on to the next.

ACKNOWLEDGEMENTS

The author and the publishers wish to thank the copyright holders for their permission to reproduce the following material:

Don Quixote by Miguel de Cervantes, translated by J. M. Cohen (Penguin Classics, 1950) copyright © J. M. Cohen, 1950. Reproduced by permission of Penguin Books Ltd.

The Tribute Money by Titian, reproduced with permission of the National Gallery, London.

Every effort has been made to obtain permission to reproduce copyright material. If any proper acknowledgement has not been made, we would invite copyright holders to inform us of the oversight.

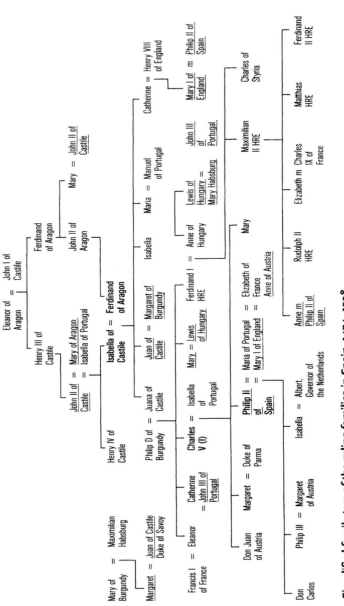

Simplified family tree of the ruling families in Spain, 1474–1598
Note: Underlined names indicate more than one appearance

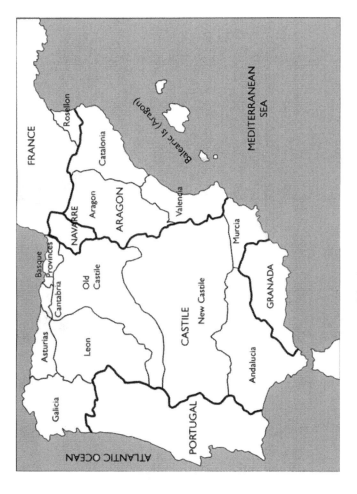

Map 1 Kingdoms and Provinces of the Iberian Peninsula, 1474

1

SPAIN AT THE TIME OF ITS 'UNIFICATION'

BACKGROUND NARRATIVE

As the twenty-first century gets under way, Spain is one of the European countries which has firmly adopted a political system based on regional self-government. This is a reminder that, until the late fifteenth and the early sixteenth century, Spain was not a single country. By the end of the sixteenth century, all the kingdoms of the Iberian peninsula had been brought together. During the sixteenth century, the King of Spain governed more of Europe than any ruler since the Romans; and at the same time, Spain became the dominant power in the New World. This book traces the history of Spain during these remarkable years, and this first chapter provides a summary of the condition of the kingdoms of Ferdinand and Isabella on the eve of their accessions.

The kingdoms of the Peninsula, in the third quarter of the fifteenth century, were Castile, Aragon, Navarre and Granada, which were to become what we now know as Spain. Castile and Aragon were brought together by the marriage of Ferdinand and Isabella in 1469 and their subsequent policies. Granada and Navarre were taken by conquest. The kingdom of Portugal remained an independent country. Although it was united with Spain in 1580, through inheritance, it was to regain its independence within sixty years. Few contemporaries predicted that the marriage of Ferdinand and Isabella would result in the permanent unification of Aragon and Castile. Through the fifteenth century it had often appeared more likely that Castile would join with Portugal. The Portuguese Avis dynasty had taken the throne during a war to resist Castilian control, but frequent marriages linked the two houses ever closer. In the event, however, it was to be Castile and Aragon which together formed the kingdom of Spain. Meanwhile, the ties binding the three provinces of Aragon were never strong and the fifteenth century saw a serious attempt by Catalonia to establish itself as an independent state. Thus both Castile and Aragon experienced civil war in the years before the marriage of Ferdinand and Isabella.

The kingdoms of Spain had been established during the long years of the *reconquista*. In the early part of the eighth century, Muslim armies swept across the narrow straits of Gibraltar and defeated the Visigothic rulers of Iberia. Although raiding parties then crossed the Pyrenees, France was never Moorish, and indeed the northern parts of the peninsula, such as Asturias, were never absorbed into Muslim Spain; it was here that the reconquest began. The rest of Iberia, however, proved much harder to reconquer. Not until the tenth century was the area known as Old Castile reconquered. The first of the Iberian kingdoms to achieve its modern boundaries was Portugal, which completed its *reconquista* with a great victory at Silves in 1249. During the next fifty years, all of the peninsula except for Granada was restored to Christianity, after 500 years of crusading against Islam. Naturally the *reconquista* was not a continuous war. There were many periods when the Christians and Muslims had lived at peace; from time to time, one of the emerging Christian provinces might ally itself with the Muslims against encroaching Christian neighbours. This long struggle determined the shape and ethos of the Spanish kingdoms and is thought to be in large measure responsible for both similarities and differences between them.

Castile was the largest of the kingdoms. It occupied two-thirds of the whole peninsula, and its population was greater than that of all the rest of the Iberian kingdoms together. The monarchs of Castile, since the 1370s, had been of the Trastámara family, a branch of which provided the Kings of Aragon. The King was chosen by God, but was expected to take the advice of 'all the best, most honest and wisest men of the land'.[1] These men met in the Cortes – representatives of the nobility, the clergy and the towns. The consent of the Cortes was needed for direct taxation, and legislation could arise from their petitions to the crown. No law could be repealed without Cortes consent, and the Cortes was entitled to give its opinion on issues of foreign policy. The powers of the Cortes were, however, limited by the fact that it could only meet when summoned by the King. The monarch also chose which nobles should attend, and which dioceses and towns should send representatives.

Other limitations on the monarch's power were more threatening. The nobility were exempt from taxation, and could not have their property confiscated for debt. The Council of Castile, which advised the King, was made up of representatives of the powerful families. Over the many centuries of the *reconquista*, noble families had acquired large estates and considerable autonomy. It has been calculated that 97 per cent of the land of Castile was owned by just 3 per cent of the population.[2] The Church had also gained much power through years of crusade, and was exempt from taxation and had its own courts. The military orders combined the devotion of the monastic order with the traditions of crusading chivalry, but by the fifteenth century they had become powers on their own account. The noble families which dominated them had under their control fortresses and private armies. Even the towns had considerable autonomy; in order to attract Christian settlers to newly conquered areas, towns had been given rights to appoint ruling councils and to control their own affairs. Many of the noble families hoped to establish a hold over the towns and their wealth.

The economy of Castile was dominated by its geography and climate. The northern provinces had soil unsuited to arable farming, and regularly imported cereals, mainly from northern Europe. Only in the south, in Andalucia, did Castile have a substantial food growing area. Here the climate was mild, and the irrigation techniques learned from the Muslims ensured good crops. Much of central Castile, on the high plateau, was suitable only for pastoral farming. Increasingly, in the fifteenth century, wool production was the dominant activity. The quality wool from the *merino* sheep was in demand in all the textile-producing areas of Europe. The extreme weather conditions and shortage of water meant that some flocks of sheep were 'walked', that is, moved from pasture to pasture over long distances. It seems possible that there were as many as 20 million sheep in Castile by the 1470s. Towns were therefore important as markets where the wool could be exchanged for the necessities of life. In the north, towns traded with the rest of Europe, and in the south, with Africa and Italy. In the heart of Castile, towns acted as gathering points for the wool and the commodities for which it was exchanged. There was little industry, however, most Castilian wool being exported in raw form for processing elsewhere, although there were textile processing works, for example in Segovia and Toledo. In Seville and the Basque ports, ship-building was beginning to develop.

Castile's population included substantial minorities. Because they had a land frontier with the Muslim kingdom of Granada, there were comparatively few *Mudejares* (Muslims living under Castilian rule) since they found it easy to migrate to join their co-religionists. there were, however, substantial numbers of *Moriscos*, or Christians of Arab origin. Many of the towns also had large Jewish communities, mainly engaged in commerce or in the learned professions of medicine and law. While they were criticised by contemporaries for not working hard in the fields, we have to remember that they were not allowed to own land, and thus could hardly be expected to take an interest in farming issues. Some Jewish families had converted to Christianity, but these *conversos* were not fully trusted. Attitudes to the non-Christian communities varied. Close contact with the Muslims of North Africa, and with the Jews of Italy meant that these sections of the community were influential in the cultural life of Castile, and in the re-introduction of the great classical works to Europe. At the University of Salamanca, study of the writings of Aristotle enabled them to be seen as useful to Christians. There were periods of great tolerance: in the thirteenth century, one church in Toledo was used by Muslims on Friday, Jews on Saturday and Christians on Sunday. Intolerance was only just below the surface, however, and any disaster, plague or defeat in war, could result in violent attacks, often orchestrated by the Church. The uneasy *convivencia* (living together) of many centuries was to be ended in draconian fashion by Isabella.

Relationships with other countries were dictated by the physical position of Castile, between her neighbours Portugal, Granada and Aragon. In the past, Castile had allied with France, to contain the ambitions of Aragon. During the great papal schism at the end of the fourteenth century, Castile and Aragon had supported opposing Popes. Border fighting was sporadic, and marriages with Portugal and Aragon that were intended to bring peace too often provided pretexts for claims to inheritance and further conflict. For example, in the civil war which preceded Isabella's accession, the King of Portugal interfered in the hope of establishing a Portuguese regency and control over Castile.

Henry IV, King of Castile from 1454, was nicknamed 'the impotent'. He had been married to Joanna of Portugal for seven years before she became pregnant, and the daughter she bore in 1462 was believed by many to be the child of the royal favourite, Beltrán de la Cueva. Many of the powerful nobles of Castile, intent on increasing their own power, refused to recognise Joanna 'la Beltráneja', demanding instead that Henry's younger half-brother Alfonso should be the heir. In the fighting which followed, noble families sided with whichever claimant they thought might better serve their interests. When, in 1467, Alfonso died, many suspected that he had been poisoned; plague seems, however, to have been the more mundane truth. The rebel nobles then proclaimed Alfonso's sister Isabella as the heir. If they hoped that the 16-year-old princess would be a pliable tool for their ambitions, they were mistaken. Henry IV was forced, by the Treaty of Toro in 1468 to recognise Isabella as his eventual heir. When Henry died in 1474, Isabella became Queen of Castile.

Five years before her accession, Isabella had married the heir to Aragon, her cousin, Ferdinand. Marriages between Castile and Aragon had been common but had not altered the hostility that these kingdoms felt for each other. In part, this hostility derived from the differences between them.

The Kings of Aragon ruled its three constituent parts separately, gaining approval from each Cortes in turn, and spending time in Catalonia, Valencia and Aragon, though they seldom travelled to their overseas possessions. The Cortes of Aragon was dominated by the nobility, since there were two houses of nobles, the Greater and the Lesser. In contrast to Castile, all nobles were entitled to attend; similarly, any town which had once been summoned had the right to attend from then onwards. Clergy attendance was fixed by custom, rather than by the King. All taxes, and all new laws were subject to Cortes approval, and their standing committee the *Diputacion del Reyno* monitored the work of the royal administration. In addition, the *Justiciar*, appointed by the King but for life, was a kind of Ombudsman, protecting the rights of the people and arbitrating in disputes with royal officials. The King's power was subject to similar limitations in Catalonia, where the Parliament was required to meet every three years, and where the representatives of nobles, clergy and towns debated and agreed new taxation and legislation. The *Diputacion* of Catalonia supervised the navy and army as well as overseeing all aspects of government. The strength of the Cortes of Valencia lay in the fact that each of the three houses could meet independently, and without royal summons, if affairs appeared to warrant it. It was possible for the three Aragonese Cortes to meet in a General Assembly, but there were few occasions when concerted actions seemed attractive to these very different kingdoms. Thus we may recognise the very limited nature of constitutional monarchy in the kingdom of Aragon, and the amount of royal energy needed to manage the jealous rivalries of its three regions.

The power of the nobility in each of these three provinces was based on large land holdings. A type of feudalism existed, which kept the peasants tied to the land by all kinds of obligations and dues. The nobles could raise substantial, if untrained, armies at need. The people of the great towns, such as Barcelona and Valencia, jealously guarded their privileges and rights. The military religious orders were, as in Castile, dominated by a few noble families. The Aragonese Church was virtually autonomous; proximity to Italy meant that the churchmen were more actively involved in curial politics, and one Aragonese family, the Borgias, rose to the Papacy itself. The Church was probably more corrupt than that of Castile, and the reformed orders, such as the observant Franciscans were less influential than they were in Castile. The great wealth of the Church appears to have encouraged corruption, and foreign visitors were struck by the high level of superstition among the common people.

The economy of Aragon had been both strong and diverse at the beginning of the fifteenth century. Commerce, through the great port of Barcelona, was highly developed: it was the Catalan maritime code that was used all over the Mediterranean, and the city maintained its own base in Bruges in the Netherlands. The major town of Valencia contained various industries, and the kingdom was fed by varied agriculture. One of the skills learned from the Moors was that of irrigation, and Aragon was almost self-sufficient in grain, though some foodstuffs were imported from their possessions in Italy. As the fifteenth century progressed, however, the trade of Barcelona suffered a decline, and the civil war did nothing to arrest this.

The ethnic minorities of Aragon were more assimilated than those in Castile. The *Mudejares* had been allowed to retain their civil and religious customs, and their technical and scientific knowledge were appreciated and imitated, both in agriculture and in industry. The Jews were less numerous, but still influential, and tolerated on the whole, although they might be subjected to mob violence, for example when plague broke out in Barcelona. Possibly as much as one-third of the population was non-Christian. In the cities of its Mediterranean coastline, the kingdom of Aragon possessed a more cosmopolitan economy and culture than did Castile.

Aragon had considerable holdings outside Spain, controlling the Balearic Islands, Sicily and Sardinia, and a branch of the dynasty ruled the South of Italy, in Naples. Ambitions in the south of Italy were to bring about a long and difficult war in the final years of the fifteenth century. During the earlier part of the century, however, the foreign policy of Aragon was focused on its own borders with Castile and with France. Marriages with Castile held together fragile truces, as did tentative alliances with Castile's traditional enemy Portugal. The second half of the fifteenth century saw civil war in Aragon, as in Castile. In pursuit of his ambition to absorb Navarre, John II (1458–79) had married the heiress Blanche. On her death, she left her own kingdom to her son, rather than her husband. The fighting which ensued almost split Aragon. Catalonia sided with the young Charles of Viana and, when he died in his father's prison, appealed for help from the King of Castile, and even offered the throne to Rene of Anjou. To ensure that France did not support the Catalan rebels, John handed over the disputed provinces of Rosellon and Cerdena; Aragonese and Spanish policy for the next century was to focus on the hope of regaining them. France remained hostile, however, and was horrified by the marriage of John II's heir Ferdinand to the newly recognised heir to the throne of Castile: Isabella. Louis XI tried hard to have the marriage annulled, and even attempted to arrange the marriage of La Beltráneja to his own brother to strengthen a French claim to Castile.

All the divisions and the hostility between the two kingdoms were neutralised, however, by the enduring marriage of the two remarkable young heirs to the kingdoms. Negotiations were carried out in secret, particularly by the great noble family of the Enríquez, and the two met for the first time in October 1469, marrying almost at once. It seems probable that Isabella was personally involved in the drafting of the marriage treaty, which ensured that the couple would live in Castile and their children reared there; and that Ferdinand would supply Aragonese troops and money to fight Castile's causes. There appears to have been no intention to unite the two kingdoms, and the contract said nothing about who would inherit in the event of one of them dying. Nevertheless, this marriage marked the beginning of the process which formed the modern country of Spain.

Table 1.1 Summary of Castile and Aragon in the fifteenth century

	Castile	Aragon
component parts	Galicia, Asturias, Basque Provinces, Leon, Andalucia, Murcia, Old Castile, New Castile	Aragon, Valencia, Catalonia
non mainland areas	Canary Islands	Balearic Islands, Sicily
population	Over 5,000,000	Probably less than 1,000,000
population minorities	*Moriscos* (Christians of Muslim ancestry); about 300,000 Jews; *conversos* (Christians of Jewish ancestry)	About 300,000 *Mudejares* (Muslims); *Moriscos* (Christians of Muslim ancestry); Jews; *conversos* (Christians of Jewish ancestry)
ruling family	A branch of the Trastámara family	A branch of the Trastámara family
Cortes	3 houses: nobles, clergy, commons (i. e. towns) could control some taxation not summoned at all 1483–97 could only meet when summoned by ruler	4 houses: Greater and Lesser nobles, clergy and commons; Valencia and Catalonia each had a Cortes as well. These could only meet when summoned by the ruler

continued

SPAIN AT THE TIME OF ITS 'UNIFICATION'

Table 1.1 continued

	Castile	Aragon
		In Aragon, the Cortes elected a *Justiciar* (for life) whose job was to look out for and protect their constitutional rights
'ruling classes'	500,000 were *hidalgos*, with exemption from taxation, torture and imprisonment for debt Council of Castile, made up of important nobility Military orders had their own armies	Nobles in Valencia and Aragon with substantial feudal powers over their 'remença' peasants; the town guilds of Barcelona were also very influential Military orders had their own armies
economic strengths and weaknesses	High quality wool was produced; but not enough wheat was being grown and the *Mesta*, the guild of sheep farmers, was getting too powerful	Strong arable production; commerce very important to Catalonia, but decline of the port of Barcelona as the focus of Mediterranean trade altered. Industrial production in Valencia: textiles and metals
main foreign policies	Tension between Castile and both Aragon and Portugal; periods of hostility interspersed with alliances and marriages. Ambition to obtain the kingdom of Navarre	Tension between Aragon and both Castile and France; periods of hostility interspersed with alliances and marriages. Ambition to take back the Pyrenean provinces of Rosellon and Cerdena

ANALYSIS (1): WHAT IMPACT DID THE *RECONQUISTA* HAVE UPON THE DEVELOPMENT OF SOCIETY IN CASTILE AND ARAGON?

The existence of separate kingdoms with very different traditions was a result of the *reconquista*. Christian communities were established as the Muslim powers were pushed back, until only Granada was left. Language differences and varied attitudes were an inevitable result of a process stretching over 500 years. Some of the earliest Christian settlements, in Basque Provinces and Asturias, spoke very different languages from those of the kingdoms further south. Because the various Christian areas had also been rivals, and had from time to time allied with the Muslims against each other, there was little trust between them. The high mountains to the north, and the surrounding seas to the east and west, give Iberia an appearance of uniformity which is not borne out by the study of its history.

The long drawn out period of crusading had enhanced the status of knightly virtues. The spirit of *reconquista* lived on into the fifteenth century When Isabella determined to finish the conquest of Granada, fighters flocked to join her armies from across the peninsula. Much of the popular literature of Spain consisted of ballads and adventure stories about the heroes of the *reconquista*, such as the saga of Amadis of Gaul. These legends can be compared to the King Arthur stories in contemporary England. In the early seventeenth century, Miguel de Cervantes created his hero Don Quixote de la Mancha as a satire on this adulation of the knightly classes. It has been suggested (for example by D. W Lomax[3]) that the spirit of *reconquista* made Castile uniquely qualified to establish a substantial overseas empire in the early sixteenth century. At the same time, however, it encouraged Spaniards to value chivalry above more mundane work, and to look for ways to achieve noble status and the privileges which would enable them to give up day-to-day employment. Thus there was a migration of productive citizens into the *hidalgo* class, where they would benefit from tax exemptions and additional privileges. 'I did not come here to till the soil like a peasant', said one of the conquerors of Mexico in the 1520s, 'but to get rich as all men desire to do.'[4]

To attract settlers to newly conquered areas, and to reward the knightly leaders, special privileges had been awarded to towns, and virtual autonomy to the holders of great estates. These privileges might include exemptions from taxation and the normal course of the law, as well as rights to self-government. One effect was to make the struggle to assert royal power even more difficult in the kingdoms of Spain than it was in contemporary England or France. Neither of these kingdoms had the Iberian military orders to contend with. A product of the crusades, just as were the Knights of the Temple, or the Teutonic Knights, these orders had become the effective property of the great noble families, who used their armies and fortresses to oppose the monarch. The Church itself was also very powerful, as might be expected after half a millennium of religious war. It held huge areas of land and dominated the educational and moral welfare of the people. It was also useful to the crown. Not only did it provide a propaganda mechanism for instruction and control, but it shared its substantial income with the government. Because of the *reconquista*, and the need to fight the infidel, traditionally one-third of all tithe paid (the *Tercia Real*) had gone to the crown. In addition, the *cruzada*, or crusading levy, could be collected. This was raised by the selling of indulgences, in theory to enable those who could not go to fight to share the spiritual benefits of those who did.

The years of *reconquista* also determined the attitude of Spain to its minority populations. Where convivencia was the practice it worked well; but underlying the tolerance was a bigotry based on fear, and focused as much on converts and their descendants as on those who had kept to the faiths of their ancestors. In the thirteenth century, an office of the Inquisition had been established in Catalonia specifically to search out converted Jews and ensure their compliance with Christian traditions.

It would be an exaggeration to say that all aspects of Iberian life were coloured or formed by the experience of the *reconquista*. Other European nations, without the centuries of crusading, had powerful and wealthy nobles, virtually autonomous religious hierarchies and an ambivalent attitude to non-Christian populations. The Jews of England, for example, had been expelled altogether in 1290.

Questions

1. Is it an exaggeration to say that every aspect of life in the Iberian peninsula was affected by the *reconquista* tradition?
2. How far was the high status of the nobility in Castile and Aragon the result of the *reconquista*?

ANALYSIS (2): WERE THE SIMILARITIES BETWEEN CASTILE AND ARAGON BEFORE THEIR UNIFICATION GREATER THAN THE DIFFERENCES?

Geographical proximity, and the fact of their eventual union into the one kingdom of Spain, makes it inevitable that comparisons between Castile and Aragon will be made. They were similar in many ways. Each was made up of several provinces, which maintained a regional distinctness and considerable local pride. Even in the twenty-first century, it is the Basque Provinces, part of Castile, that joins Catalonia, part of Aragon, in demands for local autonomy. The royal families were branches of the same clan, and had married and intermarried until papal dispensation of the prohibited degrees was needed for almost every peninsular wedding. Both found themselves involved in civil strife as the fifteenth century ended, with close relatives opposing each other and gaining support from different regions of the kingdoms.

Although in Castile the monarch was subject to far fewer, and less encompassing, legal limitations than applied in Aragon, nevertheless both kingdoms were ruled by limited monarchs. In each kingdom, the representatives of the different classes were guaranteed a certain involvement in the government, and the rulers found it necessary to placate the Cortes on occasion. In both kingdoms, the nobility had acquired excessive power, and in both the Church was in need of reform. The systems of taxation, after years of exemptions and having favoured certain classes, did not bring in sufficient revenue for the ambitious foreign and dynastic policies of the rulers. The interest of the rulers of both in the artistic developments of Flanders and Italy were also more expensive than the kingdoms could well afford.

The economies of both kingdoms had experienced changes during the fifteenth century. Several of the larger towns had suffered economic dislocation as a result of outbreaks of plague, and the pattern of agriculture was shifting, particularly in Castile, where the grazing of sheep for wool had for many years been the most profitable type of farming. The increasing population was, however, to begin the reversal of this trend during the reign of Ferdinand and Isabella, and increasing amounts of cereals were being planted. The balance of the population in both kingdoms, too, was changing: in Castile, the movement from the harsh areas of the north to the cities further south, which was to worry the rulers of the sixteenth century, was beginning. In Aragon, the population of the great city of Barcelona was shrinking as workers and professionals moved south to Valencia.

In both Castile and Aragon, the substantial ethnic minorities were vulnerable to popular hostility and to envy of their technical expertise and the resultant prosperity. Both Jews and Muslims had lived in Iberia for centuries, and, while some communities had converted, these remained distinct and recognisable, half-way between their racial group and their adopted religious group. In Aragon, however, the *Mudejares* and the Jews played important roles in civic and national government and in the economy, and so were less vulnerable than their counterparts in Castile.

While Castile had more of its population living in small towns than did Aragon, its economy was, in the main, more agrarian than that of Aragon, and this coloured the whole of society. The great noble families owned vast estates, and dominated their communities. In rural inland Aragon, the hills and rivers made communication difficult; the strength of the economy lay mainly in the coastal cities. Although the basic structures of government appear to have been similar, there were substantial differences. Each of the provinces of Aragon was accustomed to rule by an absentee, and for that reason the power of the *Diputacions* had been allowed to grow. In Castile, the monarch was expected to travel throughout the kingdom, to be accessible to the people. This constant progress was bound to change, as government became more complicated. By the time of Isabella's accession, the *Chancillería*, or High Court, had ceased to travel with the ruler, but was based permanently in Valladolid. The other institutions of government were similarly to cease to be peripatetic during the next century. These differences should not, however, obscure the fact that the two governments faced similar problems with powerful nobles, recalcitrant towns and a Church hierarchy which lay outside its control.

The most potentially divisive contrast between the two kingdoms was the focus of the foreign policy of each. Castile looked towards gaining possession of Portugal, and towards further crusading in North Africa. Aragon, on the other hand, hoped to enhance its holdings in Italy, and to increase its control of trade in the western Mediterranean. One of the many surprises of the reign of Ferdinand and Isabella was the way in which the foreign policies and resources of the two kingdoms came together in pursuit of common aims.

Castile and Aragon had no more in common with one another than, for example, did Castile and Portugal. The expectation at the time of the marriage of Ferdinand and Isabella appears to have been, as so often in the past, that the collaboration would not outlast the duration of the marriage, and that on the death of one of them the two kingdoms would again become separate. Instead, as a result of the work of the monarchs, and of dynastic problems and coincidences, Spain came into enduring existence.

Questions

1. Did dynastic marriages improve or damage the relationships between Castile and Aragon?
2. To what extent were the foreign policies of Castile and Aragon determined by their relationship with each other?

SOURCES

1. DIVISIONS AND PROBLEMS IN CASTILE

Source A: the language differences of Spain explained by comparison with those of the King of Scotland.

His own Scotch language is as different from English as Aragonese from Castilian. The King speaks, besides, the language of the savages who live in some parts of Scotland and on the islands. It is as different from Scotch as Biscayan is from Castilian.

Source B: Giucciardini's – Italian – view of Spain's problems.

... poverty is great here, and I believe it is due not so much to the quality of the country as to the nature of the Spaniards, who do not exert themselves; they rather send to other nations the raw materials which grow in their Kingdom only to buy them back manufactured by others, as in the case of wool and silk which they sell to others in order to buy them back from them as cloths of silk and wool.

Source C: the Oath of the Cortes of Aragon.

We, who are as good as you, swear to you, who are no better than we, to accept you as our King and sovereign Lord, provided you observe all our liberties and laws.

Source D: one of Isabella's historians looks back on the reign of Henry IV.

In those days, of tyrannical and thieving men and other people of evil intent, in the towns, on the roads, and generally in all parts of the Kingdom, nobody thought twice about committing any violent crime, nobody thought of obeying, of respecting, or of paying their debts to another. And for this reason, the Kingdom was full of petty thieves, crimes and violent attacks in all regions, without fear of God or of justice. And so by virtue of the present war, as well as because of the disorders and past wars of the time of Don Enrique, people were so accustomed to such disorder, that the young men assumed the customs and habits, aggressive behaviour and extravagances that youth demands, and pride and decadent customs were perpetuated in everyone's lives; in such a way that the man who showed himself the physically weakest held himself to be inferior. And the citizens, farm labourers and peace-loving men were not their own masters, nor had they recourse to anyone on account of the robberies, attacks, ransoms and other evils which they endured at the hands of the fortress lords, or other robbers or thieves. And each one volunteered to contribute the half of his goods in order to keep his person and his family safe from the threats of death, injuries or kidnappings.

Source E: an account of one aspect of the difficulties of Spanish foreign policy.

The friendship between England and Portugal dates from very old times. In case of war between Spain and Portugal, England is to remain neutral. In case of renewal of the treaties between England and Portugal, Spain is to be excepted. This is sufficient and even better than if more had been obtained. For in this manner, the friendship of both England and Portugal could be preserved. If more were said, the King of Portugal would look out for the other alliances.

Questions

*1. Explain the term 'Biscayan' (Source A). (2 marks)
2. To what extent does the Oath (Source C) give an accurate impression of the power of the Cortes of Castile in the fifteenth century? (4 marks)
3. Discuss the validity of Giucciardini's verdict 'poverty is great here' and his explanation. (4 marks)
4. How reliable do you find Source D as a description of the state of Castile in the fifteenth century? How significant is it that it was written in the reign of Don Enrique's successor? (7 marks)
5. Use your own knowledge to discuss how complete an account of the problems of fifteenth century Castile is offered by these sources. (8 marks)

Worked answer

1* *[A brief answer is, of course, enough to show that you have looked at a map of Spain, and that you understand the comparison which is being made.]*

Biscay (in Spanish, *Vizcaya*, one of the Basque Provinces) is the area, including the sea area, lying directly North of Old Castile. It is certainly a long way from the central parts of Castile, and had experienced a very different history.

2

THE DOMESTIC POLICIES OF FERDINAND AND ISABELLA

BACKGROUND NARRATIVE

The marriage settlement between Ferdinand and Isabella had agreed that they should jointly rule their two kingdoms. But there was no intention to unify Castile and Aragon. Indeed, if their daughter Joanna had proved to be fully competent as ruler of Castile after Isabella's death, it is possible that the two kingdoms would have separated again from 1504 onwards. Nevertheless, many of the policies which they adopted applied to both kingdoms, since the same issues of royal authority, public order and finance applied to both. And, as we shall see in Chapter 3, they pursued a single foreign policy.

In Aragon, the aim was to restore royal authority after the years of disorder. Ferdinand's main target was the nobility, but he was also anxious to bring under control the great city of Barcelona. In Catalonia, the Sentencia de Guadelupe of 1486 removed the 'Six Evil Customs' which had bound the *remença* peasants to the land and to their landlords. While the lords were compensated financially, noble influence in rural areas appears to have been lessened. In the urban environment of the great port of Barcelona, the problem was a self-perpetuating oligarchy of merchant families. Ferdinand introduced a lottery system for selection to public office in the city. There was no attempt, however, to bring the three provinces of Aragon closer together. The three Cortes continued to meet separately, and continued to wield more power than the Cortes of Castile.

Throughout the reigns of the Catholic monarchs, the determination of the Aragonese triple Cortes ensured that Castile was much more heavily taxed than Aragon. Royal authority could have been at risk, since the marriage settlement had agreed that the monarchs would reside in Castile. However, each of the regions of Aragon had a viceroy or governor who stood in the place of the King during his almost constant absence. In addition, Ferdinand revived the *Curia Regis*, or Royal Council, which met with the viceroys and agreed policy. The Treasurer of this council was empowered to make decisions about finance. This was, however, the limit of Ferdinand's administrative innovation in Castile. He knew better than to attempt the kind of wholesale centralisation which Isabella was implementing in Castile.

The succession dispute which Isabella had won to reach the throne had encouraged many of the nobility of Castile, in any case 'over-mighty' in terms of land holdings and private armies, to imagine that they could reject royal control. It bringing them to order, Isabella was not only ensuring her own security but improving conditions for the lower classes of her society.

At the Cortes of Madrigal in 1476, a start was made with the establishment of the *Santa Hermandad*. Many of the towns had set up *hermandades*, brotherhoods which supervised law and order and protected the local roads. Now these were linked in a 'holy' union, from which the nobility were specifically excluded. The *Hermandad* was intended to stamp out brigandage: the *grandes*, or great nobles, with their hordes of undisciplined retainers, often preyed on local travellers. The tribunals, staffed by unpaid *alcaldes*, or magistrates, were able to impose punishments of death or mutilation. They could also fine offenders, and their revenues were a source of additional finance, which, for example, helped to subsidise Columbus' first voyage. By the time the *Hermandad*'s supreme council was disbanded in 1498, Castile was mostly at peace, and travellers and traders could feel safe wherever they went. The Cortes held at Toledo in 1480 continued the reduction in noble power. An Act of Resumption repossessed half of all revenues lost from the crown since 1464. Noble influence in central government was removed by the establishment of the *Consejo Real* (Royal Council), from which the nobility were excluded. Other central councils established in this period, such as the Council of Finance and the Council of the Inquisition, also excluded the higher nobility.

It was also essential to reduce the influence wielded by nobles at the local level, and the Cortes of Toledo achieved this. The appointment of a *corregidor* to each town in Castile ensured that royal control was dominant. The functions of the *corregidores*, to supervise public order and local government, to prevent usurpations of royal power and to administer royal justice, were exercised for two years, although the period of office might be extended. At the end of each term of office, they submitted to a *residencia*, or inspection. These officials effectively put the authority of the monarch into every community, and therefore weakened the hold of the nobility, even in their own heartlands. In the event, the system did not work as well as it should have done. There was a shortage of suitably qualified men. For instance, throughout the entire reign of Ferdinand and Isabella, only fifty-one graduates of the elite law colleges in total chose to enter the administrative service.[1] Risks of corruption were increased by the difficulty in finding replacements. Gómez Martinique was *corregidor* of Toledo for thirteen years, without even the proper *residencia* every two years.[2] Although Isabella attempted to deal with this problem in the *Pragmatica* of 1500, which reiterated the two year term, corruption continued and worsened as time went on. Appeals against the decisions of the *corregidor* to the royal Chancillería in Valladolid, were possible, as were appeals against the decisions of the nobles' courts.

Isabella did not want to reduce the power of the nobles merely to have their place taken by the Cortes, or by the middle classes. Assisted by the voting of a larger than usual *servicio* at Madrigal in 1476, Isabella was able, subsequently, to avoid summoning the Cortes too frequently: between 1483 and 1497 there was no Cortes meeting. When it did meet, she exercised her power to select attendance, summoning only the town representatives, and selecting carefully which towns should be called. On occasion, only eighteen towns received summonses; thus the Cortes of Castile might consist of just thirty-six men.

Clearly, if the Cortes did not meet, the Queen had to find revenue from elsewhere. A first step had been taken at Madrigal, which had reduced the bureaucracy of the finance departments, and the imposition of order on the kingdom ensured that more of the revenues collected reached the government. Indeed, during Isabella's reign, tax revenue increased by thirty times: from 900,000 *reales* in 1474 to 26 million in 1504. Little of this new revenue came from the Cortes' taxes, the *servicio*. Instead, a *servicio* was collected at the annual meeting of the Santa Hermandad, and the *alcabalá*, or sales tax, was extended to all kinds of commodities. Indeed, controls were placed on where textiles could be sold in order to ensure that the *alcabalá de lanas y paños* could be collected. John II of Castile had fixed new rates for the border customs duties, and these were enforced for the first time in 1492. In addition, the sheep producers' union, the *Mesta*, was liable for the *servicio y montazgo*, a levy on the transit and pasturage of sheep, and government officials were sent out to prevent illegal collection by the nobles. The Queen still needed other sources of revenue; the Act of Resumption, in 1480, had increased the royal land holdings, and attempts were made to increase production from these lands. Borrowing was increasingly a preferred way of raising revenue: the sale of annuities, or *juros*, provided easy income but at a future cost of generous annual interest payments.

The monarchs also found it possible to collect revenue from the Church. Over the centuries of crusading, various payments had been authorised from the Church: the *Tercia Real*, or one-third of tithe, and the *decima*, which was one tenth of all clerical incomes. These payments were not abolished when the reconquista was completed. The sale of the special *cruzada* indulgences also brought substantial income to the crown, not all of which was spent on God's wars. The income from these – which were, unlike taxes, optional – did, however, decline from about 1500 onwards. The total revenues of the crown more than trebled during the reign of Isabella.

The Church was a matter of concern for the monarchs quite apart from the questions of revenue. From the very beginning of her reign, Isabella wanted to bring the military orders under royal control. These institutions of the crusading age were wealthy both in land and treasure, and had large numbers of members. To gain control of them would not only reduce the potential for noble control, but would make available thousands of sinecures which could be useful to the monarchs. In 1476, when the Mastership of Santiago fell vacant, Isabella ensured that her husband was appointed and the same happened to the Orders of Calatrava and Alcantara. By 1494, the orders were effectively a branch of government, although Papal confirmation was not obtained until 1523. The power and wealth of the diocesan church in Castile was also enormous, and the clergy were exempt from taxation as well as being outside the scope of the royal justice system. Many of the forty-seven bishops and archbishops of Castile were territorial grandees as well as clergymen; in some areas they had led their dioceses to support the Portuguese during the succession wars. Isabella recognised that the key to control was *Patronato*, the right of provision to bishoprics which at her accession lay with the Papacy. In 1482, the Pope accepted her suggestion for the See of Cuenca, and in 1486 acknowledged that the monarch of Castile should choose bishops in Granada. Once the principle was established, *Patronato* was bound to become a royal right, even though this did not occur until the accession of Charles I.

Isabella was also intent on improving the spiritual life of Castile, and in this aim she had strong support from her confessor Cisneros. His reform of his own order, the Franciscans, was the first step and, once he became Archbishop of Toledo and Primate of Castile (1495), he was able to turn his attention to the rest of the Church. New seminaries were set up to train priests, and the abuses to which the fifteenth-century Church was so prone were dealt with by regulation and visitation. Absenteeism and pluralism were reduced as the number of new priests increased. At the same time Cisneros' concern with the intellectual side of religious life led him to organise the production of a bible which had in parallel the original Greek or Hebrew texts and their Latin translations. Isabella shared his concern for the purity of the Church and its message, and it was for this reason that she determined on the most extreme action of her entire reign. Following the victory at Granada, she resolved to 'purify the temple' as she put it, by expelling all the Jews from Spain. It was thought that it would be easier for the *conversos* (Christians of Jewish ancestry) to maintain their faith if the temptation of the old ways was removed. While it was recognised that the loss of so many loyal, productive and skilled citizens might damage the economies of the kingdoms of Spain, the spiritual benefits were seen as outweighing any earthly losses. It is estimated that about 280,000 people left Spain. Many of them went to North Africa, or to Italy, and some to Portugal, where subsequently they suffered persecution as the Catholic monarchs put pressure on the King of Portugal as part of the various marriage settlements.

Removing the Jews was not the only economically damaging action carried out, with the best of intentions, by Isabella. Over the whole of her reign, the privileges of the *Mesta* were increased, sometimes in return for enhanced contributions to royal revenues, but also because it was thought that the production of wool was the best way to make Spain rich. Already, by 1480, an estimated 5 million sheep were owned by the members of the honourable company of the *Mesta*, and this number increased during the reign of the Catholic monarchs. Serious damage was done to local agriculture when common lands were declared to be for the use of all and not just of local people. Thus the enormous flocks of sheep which used the 'sheep walks' from one area of pasture to another were able to descend like locusts on the grazing land traditionally used by the community. In 1501, the *Mesta* gained royal recognition of any area which had ever at any time during the previous fifty years been a sheep walk, and the tenancy of any land ever used as pasture. The resulting distortion of agriculture meant that the government had to fix the corn price in 1502, and Spain was dependent on cereal imports from the early years of the sixteenth century. Much of the wool produced was exported for foreign manufacture, rather than providing employment in Castile, which again adversely affected the Spanish economy. The beginnings of trade opportunities in the New World went some way to encouraging the production of manufactured goods in Spain, but the opportunity was not seized with enthusiasm. The most positive economic achievement of the monarchs may be said to have been the standardisation of the coinages of the different kingdoms, in 1497.

Isabella and Ferdinand had had five children and so there was no reason to suppose that there would be succession problems. But they had only one son. Their daughters were married, as instruments of Ferdinand's foreign policies, into the families of Portugal, England and Burgundy–Austria. Juan, the heir, also married into the Habsburg dynasty, but his death in 1497, taken with the still birth of his posthumous son, meant that the throne of Castile would fall to Joanna, the daughter about whose mental stability there were already doubts. It may be thought that it was in Ferdinand's interest to spread rumours about the instability of his daughter. On the death of Isabella in 1504, Joanna was proclaimed queen and her Habsburg husband was proclaimed Philip I. Philip was determined to rule on his wife's behalf, and it seemed possible that Ferdinand would be restricted to ruling Aragon and Naples only. The death of Philip in 1506 changed everything. Civil unrest erupted in Castile as some nobles tried to use the opportunity to increase their power. Only the use of military force by Ferdinand brought Castile back under control. Within a few years,

Joanna was declared to be incapable of ruling, and was confined within the castle of Tordesillas, and Ferdinand took the regency for her son Charles, who had been born in 1500 and who was being brought up in Flanders. It was a measure of Castilian hostility to Ferdinand that his regency was not recognised by the Cortes until a meeting at Madrid in 1510. During the last few years of his reign, Ferdinand hoped desperately that his new wife Germaine would produce a son, or, failing that, that he would be able to have as his successor Charles' younger brother, who was being brought up in Aragon by his grandfather. In the event, however, Ferdinand's death in 1516 resulted in the accession of Charles to all the kingdoms and possessions of Spain.

The uncertainty at the end of Ferdinand's reign confirms that there had not been any real unification of the two Iberian kingdoms. Some policies had applied throughout the peninsula, but intrinsic differences remained and there is little indication that Ferdinand and Isabella had had any desire to turn their kingdoms into a single unit. The differences would reduce during the next reign, as Castile had to become accustomed, like Aragon, to an absentee monarch, but the kingdoms would retain their individuality. The Catholic monarchs had had other important priorities, in which they achieved some success: they had worked hard to reduce the power of the nobles, and to make their kingdoms truly Christian. The two analyses which follow consider these two aspects of their policies.

ANALYSIS (1): HOW EFFECTIVELY DID FERDINAND AND ISABELLA DEAL WITH THE POWER OF THE NOBILITY OF SPAIN?

The nobility in both Castile and Aragon were dangerous because they had substantial wealth and power; because they did not wish to see their authority reduced by the extension of royal control, and because the loyalty they felt to their own families was stronger than their loyalty to the crown. During the succession war in Castile both *grandes* and *hidalgos* had sided with the Portuguese claimant in the expectation of substantial rewards once 'la Beltráneja' secured the throne. In Aragon, nobles had backed the Catalan rising, and had negotiated with France. Ferdinand and Isabella needed both to obtain the loyalty of the nobles and also to reduce their power so that similar dangers did not arise in the future.

They shared these aims with many of the monarchies of Europe: we may, for example, see parallels between their actions and those of the new dynasty in England.

To an extent, the power of the nobility was being reduced by developments other than those instigated by the crown. The movement of populations to the towns reduced one of the strengths of the noble families: the number of vassals they could call upon. While some towns were controlled by nobles, the deployment of *corregidores* meant that the royal authority was dominant. By 1500, Seville had 75,000 inhabitants, Valladolid 35,000 and Burgos 25,000. 'The cities seethed with a turbulent multitude of artisans and woolworkers whose political goals were as yet inarticulate, but whose hatred of the rich could always be counted upon.'[3] The growth of an artisanal class, and of wealth and employment based on trade with the New World, which was the foundation for Seville's growth, excluded the nobility, with a few notable exceptions such as the Guzmans in Seville and the Veleisco family in Burgos. Even the payment of the *juros* (annuities), on which they increasingly relied, put the nobility into the hands of the monarchs and of their non-noble functionaries.

The nobles had enormous power at the start of the reign, however. During the fourteenth century, the monarchy had purchased support by ennobling many, and by extending the privileges of noble families. As well as tax exemptions, and honorific rights, lands had been awarded to them, and the Crown had turned a blind eye to the collection of unlawful taxes and tolls. Nobles whose lands bordered the sheep walks collected transit tolls on sheep; they instituted law courts which fined and punished local people. At the start of their reigns, Ferdinand and Isabella had been more intent on securing the support of the nobles than on reducing their powers. Lavish gifts to those nobles who had supported them were, however, matched by severe measures against those who had not. Seigneurial revenues taken from traitors were given to those who were loyal, thus ensuring their future commitment. Many of their domestic policies as their reigns progressed had the effect of reducing noble authority, whether directly or indirectly. The establishment of the *Santa Hermandad* in 1476, as well as safeguarding roads and trade for the whole population, ended many opportunities for noble brigandage; the reorganisation of local government extended royal control by putting authority into the hands of *letrados*, and few nobles had been educated to university level. Nobles were progressively excluded from high office in the Church by the same process. The proper control of the tax collecting and revenue systems may not appear to bear directly on the lives of the nobles, but their increasing reliance on the interest payments from their *juros* meant that their loyalty could be ensured by efficiency in these areas.

The reforms in central government were directly designed to reduce the power of the nobles. The new Royal Council as established by the Cortes of Toledo (1480) was to have as its members one bishop, three *caballeros* (knights) and eight or nine *letrados*, or men with legal training. Although *grandes* might attend the meetings, they were not members of the Council and so could not vote. Their right to attend court was guaranteed, but their participation in government curtailed. Similarly, the noble hold on the rich offices of the military orders was replaced by royal control. Between 1476 and 1494, Ferdinand became Master of each of the three great orders, and from then on the Kings of Spain were to hold these offices.

Machiavelli wrote at the time that the purpose of the *reconquista* had been to keep the nobles busy, and while this is clearly an over-simplification, many nobles participated with passionate commitment in the war in Granada. As was traditional, they might be rewarded by grants of newly conquered lands, though most noble families probably benefited more from the high and continuing interest returns on their loans to the government. Nobles held rank in Ferdinand's developing army, but the structure was so well defined that there was no risk of insurrection by officers.

By the end of the fifteenth century, a balance had been achieved, with royal authority well established and the rights of the common people protected from the worst depredations of the nobility. The next two decades, however, saw some changes, which particularly damaged the status of some towns, and which were to lead to the great risings of the reign of Charles I. The high cost of Ferdinand's wars led to raised taxes and increased the royal dependence on noble loans, and so the crown was less likely to take firm action against the nobility. After Isabella's death, disputes about the regency in Castile meant that Ferdinand was again willing to ignore noble encroachments. Nobles, hungry as always for land, occupied lands belonging to the municipalities. Around Segovia, thousands of people found themselves suddenly the tenants of the Marquis of Maya, Andres de Cabrera. In the north of Spain, *merindades*, or free villages, each with the traditional right to choose its own lord, found themselves swallowed by powerful seigneuries, and the beleaguered crown did nothing to prevent it.

Charles I was to find that the resentment of the towns and some rural areas would bring Spain to the brink of civil war in 1520. But when the *comuñeros* did rebel, the nobles remained loyal to the crown, and this may be seen as a measure of the success of the Catholic monarchs. The nobles had lost their power to dominate the government and, while they had preserved much of their wealth and status, they had recognised that their interests were best served by maintaining rather than threatening the crown of Spain. Thus Ferdinand and Isabella, who had acceded to their thrones in the teeth of opposition from the nobility, passed on kingdoms where the nobility could be depended on to preserve the monarchy.

Questions

1. Assess the successes and failures of Ferdinand and Isabella as monarchs of a united Spain. (EDEXCEL Summer 1998)
2. How well governed was Spain under Ferdinand and Isabella? (UCLES Summer 1997)

ANALYSIS (2): DID FERDINAND AND ISABELLA DESERVE THEIR TITLE OF THE 'CATHOLIC MONARCHS'?

Ferdinand and Isabella were given the title of the 'Catholic monarchs' by Pope Alexander VI in 1496. It is an apt title because they were deeply concerned with religious matters and prepared on occasion to place the spiritual health of their kingdoms above other, more mundane, considerations. At the same time, however, many of their policies towards the Church can be seen as part of broader policy aims, and as ways of enhancing royal power and status while reducing the influence of vested interests of all kinds, and it would not be true to say that their only motive was religious.

In January 1492, Ferdinand and Isabella finally completed the *reconquista*, removing the last vestige of Muslim control from the Peninsula. At first they guaranteed the way of life of the Moors, but within a few years a policy of forced conversion was adopted, resulting in the emigration to North Africa of many economically useful citizens. It could be argued that the Catholic monarchs regarded uniformity as an essential indicator of royal control, were it not for the fact that they were prepared to accept diversity in other aspects of life. Religious fervour was clearly the motivating force here. Meanwhile, in gratitude for their victory, they had made two devotional commitments in 1492. One, the sponsorship of Columbus, will be discussed in Chapter 3; but the other had a profound effect on the domestic life of Spain. This was the decision to expel the Jews. The concern was that the presence of practising Jews in the peninsula made it too easy for *conversos* to slip into their ancestral ways, and so lose their chance of salvation. The choice was given to the Jews of Spain, including those of Granada, to convert or leave, although there were always concerns about the genuineness of conversions. As the *converso* Solomon-ibn-Verga had said to King John II of Castile: 'It is of no use to Your Majesty to pour holy water on Jews and to call them Peter and Paul, while they adhere to their religion. . . . Know, Sire, that Judaism is no doubt one of the incurable diseases.'[4] The only possible justification for the expulsion was religious, since there were very few other benefits for Spain. Certainly, some Jewish property was confiscated by the crown, but the economic damage was substantial. In the cities, banking and finance was often in the hands of Jewish people. With their contacts throughout the Mediterranean littoral, they were important in trade; and their scientific and technical skills put them at the top of many of the learned professions.

The introduction of the Inquisition was initially part of the policy to ensure the salvation of converted Muslims and Jews, and to protect 'Old Christians' from the surreptitious influence of backsliding *Moriscos* and *Marranos*. As such, it can be seen as a 'Catholic' policy. In 1478, Ferdinand and Isabella asked permission of Rome to establish the Inquisition in Castile, and Sixtus IV agreed. Later popes were to be more hesitant, and requests to extend the Holy Office were less warmly received. Within a few years, the Inquisition had become an instrument of royal government. One of the few appointments which directly and closely linked Castile and Aragon was made in 1483, when Torquemada became Inquisitor General for both kingdoms. In the single year 1486–87, over 5,000 people were penanced; and 2,000 were burned during his tenure. Many of them were converted Jews and Muslims, but by the end of the century, the lists of offences included many more references to witchcraft, incredulity, blasphemy and unacceptable sexual practices. Meanwhile the Church courts themselves were being brought under royal control. By 1505, these controls were codified in the Laws of Toros, which stated, for example, that debtors could not claim sanctuary. This was a matter of sound government, rather than of respect for the Church.

The Catholic Church in Spain, as elsewhere in Europe, was clearly in need of reform. Some of the bishops had enormous and potentially dangerous powers. These dangers are exemplified by the Archbishop of Toledo, Alfonso Carillo, with his 20 fortified towns, 17,280 vassals and a military force of 2,000 as his escort. He had sided with Joanna 'la Beltráneja' in the succession war and had only accepted Isabella in 1476, in return for keeping all his property. In 1478, he had again backed the Portuguese invasion, and Isabella stripped him of much of his land.

Unsurprisingly, the monarchs wanted to establish royal control over such appointments, which would at the same time provide them with useful opportunities for patronage. The Segovia Agreement of 1475 stated that all new bishops should have a university education, which had the effect of excluding many from the noble families who had previously regarded high office in the Church as their property. The reform of many religious orders was also overdue. Cisneros, himself a Franciscan, rejected the practice of the rest of the European Church, by insisting that all the monasteries of the order were closed, and all Franciscans again became 'observants', following the mendicant way of life prescribed by St Francis. The lands and homes of the 'conventuals' were forfeit to the crown. While this may be seen as a worthy Catholic policy, the absorption of the Masterships of the military orders had little to do with their religious life. By the final years of the fifteenth century, the members of the orders did not have to remain celibate or conform to any rule. Isabella's concern was to contain the nobles and make use of the opportunities for patronage on a large scale.

Reform at parish level was, however, clearly a sign of Isabella's wish to help the souls of the people; in her confessor Cisneros she found a man able to move the Church away from the corruption which had been spreading. His view was that such reforms must be led by bishops of sound moral and intellectual standing, who would appoint educated and committed priests. The opening of the University of Alcalá, to educate future bishops, was followed by the establishment of seminaries to train parish priests. The new Bishops were in every sense servants of the State, with four-year contracts, wages, retirement pensions and *audiencias* to check their accounts like any other official. It is impossible to say why the sixteenth-century Reformation made so little headway in Spain. Some historians have suggested that it was due to the work of the Inquisition; but it seems as likely that in Spain many of the abuses which fed the demand for reform in northern Europe had already been eradicated.

Many of the policies of the Catholic monarchs had no religious element, however, except in the Renaissance sense that the good prince should be concerned for the welfare of the people. Reducing the power of the nobility, and ensuring sound governments in the towns, were matters of good sense in kingdoms where civil war, or at least disorder, had threatened the accessions of the monarchs. Heavy taxation, including taxes originally levied for overtly religious purposes but which now became part of ordinary state revenues, was not a popular or a particularly 'Catholic' approach. The attempts to regulate sheep farming and wool production may have been misguided, but they were designed for mundane and not spiritual reasons. The foreign wars in which Ferdinand engaged might be given a religious 'spin' but they were fought for the entirely secular motives of territorial gain and international status. A stable and orderly government may be said to have enhanced the everyday well-being of the ordinary people. Isabella's personal religious fervour informed her own life much more than it did her policies.

Questions

1. To what extent were the policies of Ferdinand and Isabella motivated by religious considerations? (AEB Summer 1998)
2. 'They pursued traditional aims by traditional policies'. Discuss this judgement on Ferdinand and Isabella. (UCLES Summer 1998)

SOURCES

1. IMPRESSIONS OF THE REIGN OF FERDINAND AND ISABELLA

Source A: Andres Bernaldez describes, in the 1480s, the reign of Henry IV of Castile.

At this juncture, envy and covetousness were awakened and avarice was nourished; justice became moribund and force ruled; greed reigned and decadent sensuality spread, and the cruel temptation of sovereignty overcame the humble persuasion of obedience; the customs were mostly dissolute and corrupt. Many people, having forgotten the loyalty and love which they owed their King, and following their own private interests, allowed the common good to decay, so that both private and public welfare perished.

And Our Lord, who sometimes permits evils to exist on the earth in order that each malefactor should be punished according to the extent of his errors, allowed so many wars to break out in the kingdom, that nobody could say that they were exempt from the ills that ensue from them; especially those who were their instigators, who saw themselves in such dangers that they sought to abandon a great part of that which they had previously held (in the confidence that they would be able to retain it) and left the vain attempts which they had made to increase their estates. . . . These wars lasted for the final ten years for which this King reigned. Peaceful men suffered much violence at the hands of new men who rose up and wrought great havoc. The King at this time spent all his treasury, and in addition to these expenses gave away without measure almost all the income from his royal inheritance, much of which was taken by those tyrants who abounded at that time; so that one who had held many treasures and bought many towns and castles fell into such need that he mortgaged many times over the income from his inheritance, merely in order to maintain himself.

Source B: Fernando de Pulgar describes, in 1485, how wonderful Isabella was.

Evil was so deep rooted that the cure was beyond all human thought, when God ... moved by mercy, gave the people their Queen and shepherd Dona Isabel ... who married the King Don Fernando of Aragon. By her diligence and government, in a very short time, all injustice was changed to justice, all pride to meekness, all wars and divisions ... to peace and quiet, so that the whole Kingdom enjoyed security. It was certainly a marvellous thing that what many men and great lords could not agree to effect in many years, one lone woman carried out in a little time.

Source C: Machiavelli's view of Ferdinand of Aragon.

If you study his achievements, you would find that they were all magnificent and some of them unparalleled. At the start of his reign he attacked Granada; and this campaign laid the foundation of his power. First, he embarked on it undistracted, and without fear of interference; he used it to engage the energies of the barons of Castile who, as they were giving their minds to the war, had no mind for causing trouble at home. In this way, without their realising what was happening, he increased his standing and his control over them. He was able to sustain his armies with money from the Church and the people and, by means of that long war, to lay a good foundation for his standing army, which has subsequently won him renown. In addition, in order to be able to undertake even greater campaigns, still making use of religion, he turned his hand to a pious work of cruelty when he chased out the Moriscos and rid his kingdom of them: there could not have been a more pitiful or striking enterprise. Under the same cloak of religion he assaulted Africa; he started his campaign in Italy; he has recently attacked France. Thus, he has always planned and completed great projects, which have always kept his subjects in a state of suspense and wonder, and intent on their outcome.

Source D: Cipher and code letter to Puebla, Ambassador to England, from Alvarez, Secretary of State, 28 December 1499.

The news from Spain is that the King and Queen, our Lords, have been in Aragon, and have concluded in person their parliament in Aragon, which has voted a good number of troops for three years. They have come to this town of Tortosa, where they hold the Corts of Catalonia; and in San Matteo, seven leagues from here, sit the Corts of Valencia. It is expected that they will obtain here in a very short time, more troops than in Aragon, perhaps three times as many and likewise for three years. They have already five thousand lances, most of them men-at-arms. They will further assemble, in the month of March in Castile, twenty thousand lances, ten thousand men-at-arms, ten thousand horsemen and one hundred thousand foot. May God give peace to Christendom and may these troops be employed against the infidels.

Questions

1. Explain the identity of Machiavelli, author of Source C. (2 marks)
*2. What does Source D tell you about the way in which the Provinces of Aragon were governed during the reign of Ferdinand? (3 marks)
3. Compare Sources A and B. How far do they agree about the problems which confronted Isabella at the start of her reign? (5 marks)
4. How accurate is Source C in summarising the achievements of Ferdinand? (7 marks)
5. In the light of your other knowledge, consider the extent to which *each* of these sources may be regarded as propaganda rather than accurate information. (8 marks)

Worked answer

*2. *[Remember, as always, to answer briefly but clearly, ensuring that you offer enough points for the three marks available.]*

Firstly, the source indicates the plural nature of the kingdom of Aragon: the monarchs are attending the Cortes in each of the three provinces or sub-kingdoms in order to obtain the troops that they need. From this, we can see the amount of travelling required to combine personal government with geographically diverse possessions. There is also an indication that the various assemblies are happy to comply with the requests of Ferdinand: this was not always the case in Aragon; during the reign of Ferdinand's father, the Cortes of Catalonia had stood against the wishes of the monarch. The source also indicates the reliance of the King on the Cortes for extraordinary funding, as, in this example, for the expenses of war.

2. MUSLIMS AND JEWS IN THE REIGN OF FERDINAND AND ISABELLA

Source E: letter from Isabella and Ferdinand to the Moorish King, November 1491.

Their Highnesses and Their successors shall forever permit [the] King . . . his officials and all the population, great or humble, to live by their own law, and They shall not allow their mosques to be taken from them, nor their towers and muezzins; income reserved for these things shall not be touched; nor shall their existing customs be interfered with. Moors will be judged according to their law and according to their own justices. . . . And all Moors wishing to leave for Barbary or other lands shall be given free and safe passage by Their Highnesses, along with their families, moveable goods, merchandise, jewels, gold silver and all types of arms except for powder weapons. To expedite their passage, Their Highnesses shall provide ten large ships which for a period of seventy days shall wait in the appropriate ports and then carry them free and safely to the Barbary ports. . . . Neither their Highnesses, nor their son Prince Don Juan, nor those who succeed them, shall ever order their Moorish vassals to wear badges on their clothing as the Jews do. . . . Their Highnesses will not permit Jews to have any authority over Moors, nor may they collect any rent from them. . . . No person shall be allowed to maltreat by word or deed those Christians who have become Moors, and if such renegades are the wives of Moors they will not be forced against their will to return to Christianity, but they will be interrogated in the presence of Christians and Moors and their wishes respected; the same shall apply to the children born of a Christian woman and a Moor. . . .

Source F: letter from Ferdinand to the Count of Aranda, 31 March 1492.

The Holy Office of the Inquisition, seeing how some Christians are endangered by contact and communication with the Jews, has provided that the Jews be expelled from all our realms and territories, and has persuaded us to give our support and agreement to this, which we now do, because of our debts and obligations to the said Holy Office; and we do so despite the great harm to ourselves, seeking and preferring the salvation of souls above our own profit and that of individuals.

Source G: a casualty of the expulsion of the Jews is described by the Portuguese.

Before arriving at Calicut they found two Moorish ships loaded with spices and drugs which were going to Mecca. . . . On one of these ships, he [the Captain] found a Jewess from Seville who said she had fled, on account of the Inquisition, from Spain to Barbary, and then to Alexandria in Egypt and from there to Cairo and India.

Source H: message to the Spanish Ambassador in London, 18 August 1493.

Certain Jews who have left the dominions of Spain have seized the sum of 428,000 *maravedis* belonging to Diego de Soria and in the keeping of Fernan Lorenzo, alleging that Diego de Soria owes them certain sums on bills of exchange which were given to them when they were expelled from Spain. These Jews have forfeited their rights for they carried away prohibited goods and Diego de Soria has been ordered to pay the said bills of exchange into the Royal Exchequer.

Questions

1. Explain the geographical positions of Barbary (Sources E and G), Calicut and Mecca (Source G). (3 marks)
2. How reliable as evidence do you find Source G? (3 marks)
*3. To what extent do these sources indicate that the Jews of Spain were treated unjustly? (5 marks)
4. Use your knowledge and a detailed consideration of Source E to explain why, by the end of the century, the Moors felt that they had been betrayed. (6 marks)
5. Consider the view that these sources, taken together, provide adequate evidence that Ferdinand and Isabella fully deserved their title of the 'Catholic monarchs'. (8 marks)

Worked answer

*3. *[It is essential to point out the difference between religious views then and modern attitudes, so that you avoid anachronism.]*

Source F suggests that Jews were a threat to the salvation of Christians. This seems improbable, since Judaism has never been a proselytising religion, although it may be true that *conversos* found it easier to revert to Jewish ways while there were Jews in Spain. This is an inaccurate and therefore unjust excuse for the expulsion. The fear inspired by the Inquisition is clearly shown by Source G, although in the fifteenth century the use of compulsion to 'save souls' was more acceptable than it is in modern times. A comparison of Sources E and H indicates the unequal treatment of the Jews compared to the Muslims. Confiscation of property was one of the many injustices imposed on the Jews, whereas the

Muslims who chose to leave were allowed to carry their wealth with them. Above all, the King of Granada had been defeated in war, whereas the Jews had lived peacefully and constructively in Spain since Roman times, and thus their expulsion was unjust.

3

HOW SUCCESSFUL WERE THE FOREIGN POLICIES OF FERDINAND AND ISABELLA?

BACKGROUND NARRATIVE

Throughout the reigns of Ferdinand and Isabella, Aragon and Castile pursued foreign policies which were assertive and positive. Such policies, if successful, might have been expected to enhance the status of the monarchs, as well as extending their territory and trade opportunities. The risk of future foreign attacks would have been reduced as Spain's reputation as a dominant and victorious power increased. On the other hand, defeat would have had a deleterious effect on the international standing of Spain, and, whether successful or not, aggressive foreign policies would have cost a great deal of money, and may thus have alienated public opinion at home at precisely the same time as the attention of the government was diverted abroad. This was certainly the experience of Charles, the successor of the Catholic monarchs. Both Isabella and Ferdinand inherited thrones which were under threat from foreign powers, and their first priority was bound to be to settle their own borders.

The marriage of Isabella and Ferdinand removed one of the traditional focuses of Iberian foreign policy. The two kingdoms no longer threatened each other, and their common border ceased to need armed forces to maintain it. It is possible to discern 'a new community of interest which Castile and Aragon had not previously enjoyed'.[1] The traditional approaches of the two kingdoms seemed to blend well together. The Castilian commitment to 'territorial conquest, personal endeavour and religious zeal'[2] complemented the Aragonese desires to regain territory to which the Trastámara family had a claim, and to enhance and protect their Mediterranean trade. The combined strength of the two kingdoms was substantial. The diplomatic network which Ferdinand spread across the courts of Europe was staffed mostly by men of Castilian training. The intelligence gathered from these men was often slow in arriving, and not always reliable; for example, it was not uncommon for five or six copies of the same letter to be sent by different routes to ensure its arrival, as happened during the negotiations with England following the death of Prince Arthur. Despite these problems, however, the work of his diplomats often allowed Ferdinand to take advantage of detailed inside information in his negotiations.

In the same way, the 'new' army which Ferdinand developed, under his General Gonzalo Fernandez de Córdoba, was in part both recruited and paid for in Castile. While this army was not large, it was mostly permanent and professional. This was expensive, but the Cortes and other authorities in the Iberian kingdoms provided the money without protest. One reason for this was Ferdinand's many successes; another was his willingness to 'sanctify' his various wars with religious motives. But it was also because a permanent army was less disruptive to society than the earlier conscripted peasant armies, which removed men from their communities and their regular work.

Portugal was the first focus of the combined foreign policies of the monarchs. Portugal's support for the opposition to Isabella meant that war gripped the border regions for the first five years of Isabella's reign. In 1479, however, the Treaty of Alcacovas recognised Isabella's claim to the throne. While it provided security for Portugal's Atlantic and African holdings, as far as Ferdinand and Isabella were concerned a secure western frontier had been achieved. A series of royal marriages consolidated the peace. In 1490, Prince Afonso of Portugal married Isabella, daughter of the Catholic monarchs and, on his death, the new heir Manuel married the widow. Her death resulted in the marriage in 1500 of Manuel to another daughter of Spain, Maria. It was these marriage alliances that were to lay the basis for Philip II's claim to the throne of Portugal in 1580.

Much more glorious, in contemporary eyes, than the settlement with Portugal was the completion of the *reconquista*. Ferdinand had, in 1481, echoed his wife's determination to conquer Granada, and the opportunity came in 1482 when a family feud split the ruling Nasrid House, with one faction appealing to Castile for help. The motives were not, of course, purely religious. Machiavelli suggested at the time that it was a way of keeping potentially insubordinate nobles busy; but a desire to tap into the rich trade of the North African coast may well have been as significant. The war lasted longer than might have been expected, given the divisions within Granada and the failure of the Moors of North Africa to send material assistance. Not until January 1492 did the city of Granada itself fall. The well-fortified and defended towns had to be besieged one by one, with Malaga falling in 1487 and Almería in 1489. Ferdinand and Isabella were strongly supported in this campaign. Not only did volunteers come to Spain from all over Europe to join the crusade, but within Spain, the military orders and the Santa Hermandad provided large and continuing contributions, both of money and men (for example, the Order of Santiago supplied and equipped over 1,750 cavalrymen). Money was also needed, and all sources were tapped. As well as direct borrowing, the monarchs sold *juros*, and imposed taxes on Jewish communities and on the Santa Hermandad. They were also able to benefit from two papal grants. First, since 1479, the sale of indulgences (called *cruzadas*) had been authorised to raise money for the crusade. Then, in 1482, the Pope granted them the right to the *Tercia Real*, or royal third of all tithes and of the income of Spanish benefices. We may note that the final victory over Granada did not mark the end of these two sources of revenue. Instead, they continued to be collected, because Spain was determined to carry the crusade into North Africa, if not further. As late as 1510, Ferdinand declared: 'The conquest of Jerusalem belongs to Us, and We have the title of that Kingdom';[3] and although there was no campaign in the Holy Land, the campaign in North Africa preoccupied Ferdinand for much of his reign. Moorish pirates threatened the sea links to the Balearic Islands, as well as to Naples and, from the 1480s on, they were joined by the Ottoman Turks whose navies attacked Rhodes, Malta and even Sicily. Any land gained in North Africa would also have the effect of reducing Portuguese trading influence, and there was a possibility that colonisation might ease the problem of land shortage in Castile, where huge areas, for example the province of Estremadura, were, as the name implies, of limited fertility. In the event, however, Ferdinand established no more than coastal garrisons, for example at Mers el Kebir (1505), Oran (1509), Tripoli and Algiers (1510). These outposts were vulnerable to attack from corsairs, and were to be a source of anxiety to Charles during his reign.

If interest in North Africa was one immediate consequence of the capture of Granada which could have been predicted, the sponsorship of Columbus to discover a short route to Asia was unexpected. In her gratitude to God, Isabella was more prepared to listen to Columbus than she had been in 1486. In the event, Columbus' four exploring journeys reached only the West Indies and the mainland of Central America. By the time of Isabella's death, concerns about the treatment of the native peoples were beginning to be expressed, and in 1512 the first attempts at government regulation, the Laws of Burgos, were promulgated. As was the case with so much of Ferdinand's foreign policy, his successor, Charles was to find this a growing and intractable problem throughout his reign.

Matters closer to home engaged the attention of the Catholic monarchs even before Columbus' first departure. The provinces of Rosellon and Cerdena, in the Pyrenees between France and Aragon, had been occupied by France since 1462. Ferdinand, as ruler of Catalonia to whom they had previously belonged, was determined to repossess them. He was able to make an alliance with Henry VII of England in 1489 (at Medina del Campo). Henry's accession to the throne of England had been materially assisted by the Duke of Brittany, and so Henry was angered by a French attack on his childhood protector. Although the treaty with Spain supposedly concerned Brittany, Ferdinand attacked the Pyrenean provinces and was recognised as their ruler by the Treaty of Barcelona (1493). Ferdinand's other claim in the Pyrenees concerned Navarre. During the unrest in Aragon which preceded Ferdinand's accession, Navarre had declared its independence, but there was a dispute between the families of de Foix and d'Albret over which should rule. In 1506, Ferdinand married Germaine de Foix, to enhance his claim, and to prevent the King of France gaining control of her; but he did not take action until 1512, when he was again at war against France. He demanded the right to use Navarre as a springboard for his attack into France, and d'Albret's refusal provided him with the excuse he needed to annex Navarre, which remains Spanish to this day.

Conflicts with France were a constant element in the foreign policies of Spain. The most serious and extended conflict began in 1494 with the invasion of Italy by Charles VIII. The target was the huge kingdom of Naples, which extended over the whole of southern Italy, and which had been ruled by a branch of the Aragonese royal family. When, in 1494, Duke Ferrante died, Charles decided to impose his own claim, and by February 1495 France had occupied Naples. Ferdinand was able to organise a league against France and, because French troops had done damage as they passed through the papal states, it could be called the Holy League. It consisted of Spain, England, Milan, Venice, the Papacy and the Holy Roman Empire. Such a weighty alliance was enough to persuade France to abandon Naples. For three years, Ferdinand effectively controlled Naples, but in 1500 he agreed, with the new King of France, Louis XII, to partition the kingdom. Border clashes between the Spanish south and the French north gave Córdoba the excuse, in 1503, to take over all of Naples, which remained Spanish until the eighteenth century.

One reason why Louis let Naples go was that he wanted to concentrate on France's hopes of taking the Duchy of Milan. Nominally a vassal state of the Holy Roman Empire, Milan was economically important, as it commanded the southern end of the transalpine trade routes. The double marriages between Spain and the Holy Roman Empire were also clearly anti-French in intention: during 1496–97, Juan, the son and heir of the Catholic monarchs, had married the daughter of Maximilian, while their daughter Joanna had married Philip of Burgundy, Maximilian's heir. Similar marriage ties bound the kingdom of England to the anti-French alliance. The marriage of the English heir Arthur to Ferdinand's daughter Catherine had taken place, after years of negotiation, and the death of the Prince had not ended the alliance, since Catherine was then promised to the new heir Henry, the marriage taking place in 1509. Unsurprisingly, Louis disliked this threat of hostile encirclement. But when he occupied Milan, he triggered the formation of another Holy League (1509), this time without the participation of Venice. The French were forced out of Milan in 1513. Ferdinand's apparent triumph was reversed in 1515 when the new King of France, Francis I, took Milan. More than twenty years of Spanish military involvement in Italy had failed to produce stable control, and the Italian wars were to continue in various forms for the greater part of the next fifty years.

Ferdinand had achieved some, but not all, of his ambitions. The policies discussed in council in both Castile and Aragon had, in large measure, been implemented. The territory of Spain had been extended, and Spain's reputation stood high in Europe. But not all issues raised in the wars of the Catholic monarchs had been settled, and the costs of the foreign policies adopted would be felt by Spain's finances for many years to come.

ANALYSIS (1): WITH WHAT AIMS DID FERDINAND BECOME INVOLVED IN WARS IN ITALY?

At its most obvious level, Spain's involvement in Italy was a matter of regaining territory taken from the Trastámara family. Naples had been a part of the lands of Aragon until the accession of Ferrante in 1458, and so it is not surprising that Ferdinand was reluctant to see it in the hands of France. It is, however, an oversimplification to suggest that the wars in Italy were merely a matter of family pride.

Italy had long been, and remained, at the centre of Europe's commercial life. Sicily produced grain which was increasingly needed as Iberian farmers turned to sheep production. The trade of the East and of the Mediterranean flowed through Italy, and possession of lands in Italy ensured participation in this wealth. Aragon, far more than Castile, was involved in Mediterranean trade, and her island possessions encouraged this. But Ferdinand would not have gone to war in Italy merely to extend his trading opportunities, or to procure grain, had he not had other motives. He had, for example, a modern and professional army, which had been tested in Granada. Among the innovations made by Ferdinand and his military commander de Córdoba were a small force of arquebusiers (hand gunners) and a substantial number of lightly armed and highly trained pikemen. The preferred method of attack, as applied in Granada, Italy and subsequently in the Pyrenees, began with an intense artillery bombardment to breach defensive walls or emplacements. Then the pikemen and crossbowmen would lead the assault, with the arquebusiers in support, almost as snipers, to pick off the enemy leaders. The small troops of cavalry would then chase and harry the retreat. In Italy, this army confronted and fought alongside the hired mercenaries of both France and the Italian states. Ferdinand was able to demonstrate that a genuine 'national' army could hold its own with the *condottiere* who earned their livings by selling their military skills. Status and glory were bound to result from successful campaigns against the might of France.

The main reason for Ferdinand's involvement in Italy was, however, a determination to reduce or at least limit the power of France. The rivalry between Aragon and France was long lived, although France had tended to side with Castile in conflicts against Portugal and its English allies. Throughout his reign, Ferdinand engaged in a series of alliances whose central aim was to weaken and intimidate France. The marriage alliances, while seldom directly linked to conflict with France, had the effect of reducing the opportunities for the French royal family to forge similar links. Three marriages with Portugal made it difficult for France to stir up the old rivalries on Castile's western frontier. The double marriage with the Habsburg family of 1496–97 demonstrated a clear anti-French bias, since the lands of Burgundy were the subject of a strong claim by France. And the prolonged negotiations with England, France's oldest enemy, resulted in the marriage of the two successive heirs to the throne to the Spanish Princess Catherine. Even the last marriage of Ferdinand's reign, his own to the young Navarrese claimant Germaine de Foix in 1506, was directly anti-French in intent. Much more so were his alliances at Medina del Campo in 1489 (with England), and his two 'Holy Leagues' of 1495 and 1509. It was only to be expected that France should view this hostile network with anxiety and seek where possible to fracture it by separate negotiations and peace making.

The first point of conflict was in the Pyrenees, and this was to remain a focus of Spanish–French rivalry throughout Ferdinand's reign. The provinces of Rosellon and Cerdena were Catalonian until the French occupation of 1462, and Navarre, although independent for many years, could not really expect to remain so given its position between two of the most powerful nations in Europe. At the Treaty of Barcelona (1493), which recognised his possession of Rosellon and Cerdena, Ferdinand had acknowledged France's 'just claims in the realm of Naples', claims which dated from the thirteenth century, and the papal donation to Charles of Anjou, brother of St Louis. But a palliative statement in a treaty which had otherwise given Ferdinand all he wanted was not the same as actually conceding the rich trading opportunities of Naples. Having defeated the French on his own borders, Ferdinand was confident that he could do the same in Italy, and that was the main motive for his involvement.

The alliance formed in 1495 may have been called the 'Holy League', but the Spanish taking of Naples was by no means a crusade. Naples became the only part of Spain's empire where Jews were allowed to live, and trade with Muslim North Africa continued under Ferdinand's rule. The invasion of Italy was not an extension of the *reconquista*.

It is possible to recognise a valid Spanish claim to Naples, but the same cannot be said of Milan. Ferdinand's involvement in the conflict in north Italy had as its main focus the rivalry with France. The French occupation of Milan in 1509 was a demonstration of intent, and a potential threat to the other small and divided princedoms and duchies of Italy. It was easy to bring together another Holy Alliance, because the Papacy continued to be concerned about French ambitions for the Italian peninsula. The new young King of England was anxious to demonstrate his prowess, and to spend his inheritance, and so was prepared to send his troops to harry France while Ferdinand engaged the main French strength in north Italy. It seems unlikely that Ferdinand ever thought that he would hold Milan for himself, although after the expulsion of France in 1513, Spanish troops did occupy the city. This was not a piece of territorial aggrandisement, but an attempt to prove Spanish superiority over the French. In the last year of Ferdinand's life that superiority was brought into question by the striking French victory at Marignano (1515) which retook Milan.

Italy was not Ferdinand's main focus. The states of Italy became merely the theatre in which he chose to play out his rivalry with France. The Spanish hold on Naples was indeed assured, but at great expense. Claims in north Italy were not particularly valid ones, and Milan was no more than an extravagance. But France was bound to be alarmed at the strength of a united Spain; and when, on Ferdinand's death in 1516, that strength was added to the Habsburg and imperial power, France was clearly in great danger. Thus Ferdinand's Italian wars were merely the first manifestations of a conflict that was to convulse Europe and damage both sides so much during the first half of the sixteenth century.

Questions

1. 'The invasions of Italy in 1494 did not create the disunity of Italy: they merely confirmed it.' Discuss this comment. (EDEXCEL Summer 1998)
2. Discuss the view that Ferdinand's foreign policy was over-ambitious considering the many problems confronting Spain at home.

ANALYSIS (2): HOW TRUE IS IT THAT CASTILE'S SPONSORSHIP OF OVERSEAS EXPLORATION WAS MOTIVATED BY RIVALRY WITH PORTUGAL?

Rivalry with Portugal was so much an integral part of Castilian policy that it would have been remarkable to find any aspect of foreign affairs untouched by it. It had been Castile's attempt to take over Portugal which had ensured the accession of the illegitimate – and anti-Castilian – House of Avis in 1385. The civil strife which plagued the early years of Afonso V in the 1440s was encouraged in Castile. In the 1460s, Isabella's claim to the throne was resisted by the Portuguese, who would have preferred Joanna 'la Beltráneja' to be Queen of Castile.

Overseas exploration had been dominated by Portugal since the first ships were sent south by Prince Henry 'the Navigator' in 1418. By the time Isabella came to the throne, Portugal had colonised the island groups of Madeira and the Azores, and had coasted Africa to the equator. The gold, ivory and slaves of Guinea (West Africa) meant that merchants were prepared to continue the exploration in return for trading rights. By his journey of 1487, which reached the southern tip of Africa, Bartholomew Diaz demonstrated that the route to Asia was open. Isabella might well have wished to prevent Castile's old rival benefiting from the immense wealth which the oriental trade would bring.

Already in 1479, Isabella had signalled her interest by restating Castile's claim to the Canary Islands in the Treaty of Alcacovas. Preoccupied with establishing her authority at home, however, she had accepted Portugal's claims to Africa and the other Atlantic islands. Now, in 1492, came the chance to race Portugal to Asia. The Genoese Columbus had been seeking sponsorship since 1486. His ideas appeared to be soundly based in the geographical knowledge of the time. According to the book of Genesis, the world consisted of one land mass, so the eastern coast of Asia lay to the west of Europe. The world had been known, since the time of the Greeks, to be spherical, and some calculations suggested a diameter of 12,000 miles. Given the huge eastward extent of Asia, as reported by Marco Polo in the thirteenth century, the Atlantic must therefore be very narrow, and Cathay close to Europe. Isabella was impressed by these arguments, and was undeterred by the fact that the Portuguese, with their years of acquired expertise, had rejected Columbus on the grounds that his figures were wrong. Looking for some way to thank God for the triumph at Granada, and aware that Columbus had other sponsors who would cover most of his costs, Isabella accepted the symbolism of Columbus' first name, and agreed that he should 'carry Christ' to the heathen in China and Japan. A distinct religious and crusading motive can thus be discerned, although this, too, was tinged with a wish to outdo Portugal. Castile had, since the papal schism of the fourteenth century, considered that Portugal was insufficiently committed to the true Church. As part of the marriage alliances, Portugal was meant to enforce the same anti-Jewish policies as had Spain, but the Portuguese monarchs were reluctant to lose such a talented and useful part of their population and in fact delayed and evaded the commitment: Jewish communities suffered discrimination, but not expulsion.

Following Columbus' first voyage, the Pope was asked to decide which of the European countries should have the duty of conversion and the rights of trade in different parts of the world. Since he was Aragonese, it is not surprising that Alexander VI's Bull *Inter Cetera* (1493) should favour Spain; determined negotiation by the Portuguese resulted in the Treaty of Tordesillas (1494) which moved the line of demarcation 300 leagues (2,100 miles approximately) further west, thus guaranteeing Portugal's preferred routes south through the Atlantic and, incidentally, giving Portugal an entitlement in South America, which was to become its colony: Brazil. The future history of colonisation was to be the arena for constant accusations by either country that the other was failing to fulfil the obligations of conversion.

When the Portuguese da Gama reached India, by sailing south and west around Africa, he is said to have explained that he came to seek Christians and spices. The trade of Asia was a prize worth competing for, not merely against Portugal but for its own sake. Aragon's involvement in the south Italian lands had ensured a share of the trade, but this trade had been reduced by Moorish piracy and by the expansion of Ottoman power. More and more of the goods which reached Venice by the traditional routes were being forwarded overland, through Burgundian territories, or direct by fast Venetian galley to Flanders. The marriage ties which the Catholic monarchs forged with the Habsburgs did not guarantee a share in the trade, and thus there were valid economic reasons to find a new route to the source of the textiles, spices and other luxuries of the East. As Spanish wool production increased, markets abroad were also necessary, and Castile's hope was that the silks and cottons of Asia would be exchangeable for the heavier textiles of Europe. In the event, the land that Columbus discovered provided a huge market for Spanish woollens for, until Peru was occupied, the Spanish areas of America were without large pastoral animals at all.

Wealth and religious success were both sound reasons for Isabella to be enthusiastic about Columbus, but her investment was never large. Some public money was forthcoming, but much of the capital was put forward by private backers, the royal sponsorship being more in the form of guarantees, and facilitation in dock yards and supply bases. Comparatively few of the 'Spanish' explorers were actually from Castile. Columbus himself had been living in Portugal for some years before his first voyage, and in 1499 the Catholic monarchs contracted with the Florentine Vespucci to explore what Columbus had discovered. While a passing concern was expressed over the treatment of the native peoples, the lands in the New World were never at the centre of Spanish policies. They had been discovered accidentally, and Isabella's initial involvement had been almost fortuitous. It was true that any participation in overseas exploration must be anti-Portuguese, since only Portugal was active in the field. The triumphalism of the letter to King John II describing Columbus' landfall in Asia is matched only by the complacent tone of the letter by which King Manuel informed the Castilian Queen of da Gama's arrival in Calicut, India. Overall, however, Isabella's motives were as much concerned with her religious faith and with economic interests as with rivalry with her neighbours. After the 1479 peace with Portugal, it was important for Spain's domestic calm, and for the furtherance of policies elsewhere in Europe, that the western frontier should remain a peaceful one.

Questions

1. To what extent was Spain's domination of Latin America throughout the sixteenth century begun by accident?
2. How important were dynastic considerations in the foreign policy of Ferdinand and Isabella?

SOURCES

1. PROBLEMS IN THE CONDUCT OF FOREIGN POLICY

Source A: unreliability of ambassadors, hinted at in a letter of Ferdinand and Isabella to Puebla, Ambassador to England, 10 January 1497.

We believe what you affirm, that it is not your fault that you have not written to us for so long a time, notwithstanding that so many English ships have arrived by which we have received nothing; nor any answer from you to the many letters which we have written to you. Six or seven months having thus passed away without hearing, we had good reason to think the blame was yours.

Source B: difficulties of communication around Europe described in a letter of Sanchez Londona, Ambassador to England, to Ferdinand and Isabella, 10 January 1497.

I could not send a carrier from England by sea because the weather was too boisterous. The messenger of Don Pedro de Ayala went with them, first to Calais and Brussels and then to a seaport in Flanders, whence he embarked for Spain.

Source C: part of the Indenture of the Marriage of Catherine and Arthur, 7 July 1488.

Either of the contracting parties is to assist the other when attacked by an enemy; the party who demands assistance to pay the expenses. Rebels of one contracting party are not to be permitted to stay in the dominions of the other contracting party. If one of the contracting parties conclude a treaty with other princes, the other party is to be included in the nomination.

Source D: letter from Ferdinand and Isabella to Puebla, 17 December 1488.

After the conclusion of the alliances the King of England shall bind himself to make war upon the King of France, every time and whenever Spain is at war with France and whenever he is requested to do so; also he shall not be at liberty to make peace or alliance with France, or any truce, without our express consent, except the King of France do really give back to the King of England the Duchies of Guienne and Normandy. In that case, the said King of England is at liberty to conclude peace and alliance with the King of France. In the same way, we bind ourselves to make war on the said King of France every time and whenever the said King of England is at war with France, and we are requested by others to do so, and will make no peace or alliance with the King of France or assent to any truce without his consent except the said King of France give back to us our counties of Rosellon and Cerdaña in which case we will be at liberty to conclude peace and alliance with France.

Source E: letter from King Ferdinand to Queen Elizabeth of England, 4 December 1489.

The King Ferdinand has conquered the town of Baca in the Kingdom of Baca in the Kingdom of Granada and has made great progress in the war against the Moors. As this victory must interest all the Christian world, he thinks it his duty to inform the Queen of England of it.

Questions

1. Explain who Queen Elizabeth was (Source E). Why is it surprising that the letter is addressed to her? (2 marks)
2. Explain why the marriage indenture (source C) included provisions to prevent rebels of one signatory party taking refuge in the lands of the other. (4 marks)
3. What impression do you obtain from Sources A and B of the difficulties of diplomacy in the fifteenth century? (5 marks)
*4. How probable was it that the conditions laid down (in Source D) for unilateral peace with France would ever be met? (6 marks)
5. How complete an impression of Spain's foreign policy can be obtained from these sources? (8 marks)

Worked answer

*4. [It is important to show that you know the background to the various territorial claims referred to in the agreement.]

One problem with alliances was the risk that one signatory might make peace with the enemy without consulting others. By this agreement, England is bound not to make peace without Spain unless Guienne and Normandy are first returned. This would never happen. Although both areas had in the past been ruled by England, and both formed part of the formal title of the King of England, they were, by this stage, integral parts of the French kingdom, and would never have been returned. Rosellon and Cerdena (Cerdaña) were a less clear-cut issue and indeed, by the Treaty of Barcelona (1493) the two areas were returned to Aragon. They had been taken by France only in 1462, during the conflict between Catalonia and Aragon, and were predominantly Iberian by culture and tradition. Thus the terms of the treaty are very uneven, and the ambitions of Henry VII were not realistic.

SOURCES

2. THE SIGNIFICANCE IN EUROPE OF EARLY OVERSEAS EXPLORATION

Source F: the ultimate destination of the spices.

And thus ten ships, having arrived laden, left for Lisbon, the eighth of December of that year 1502. And on their way back one of them got lost. We have heard that it got lost by the coast of the Land of Santa Cruz. The others arrived in safety on the 1st of September 1503 with many spices. If God wills it, we intend to send a ship with these spices by the coast of Spain and another by the coast of Italy up to Venice so that it may be known that both our armadas and our expenses are not thrown to the wind.

Source G: Antonio de Nebrija, court poet and historian, writes (1496) about the reputation of the Catholic monarchs.

And now, who cannot see that, although the title of the Empire is in Germany, its reality lies in the power of the Spanish monarchs who, masters of a large part of Italy, and the Isles of the Mediterranean Sea, carry the war to Africa and send out their fleets, following the course of the stars, to the Isles of the Indies and the New World, linking the Orient to the western boundary of Spain and Africa.

Source H: Hernando Columbus explains the implications of his father's second voyage.

In order to make their title clear and good, the Catholic Sovereigns, on the Admiral's advice, very promptly applied for the Supreme Pontiff's confirmation and gift of the conquests of all these Indies. The reigning Pope, Alexander VI, most liberally granted them not only all they had conquered so far, but also everything that they should still discover further west as far as the Orient . . . and forbade all others to encroach on these boundaries.

Source I: Christopher Columbus emphasises his achievement.

Those who have opposed this excellent enterprise . . . do not take into consideration that the Princes of Spain have never gained possession of any land out of their own country until now, that your Highnesses have become the masters of another world, where our holy faith may become so much increased, and whence such stores of wealth may be derived; for although we have not sent home ships laden with gold, we have nevertheless sent satisfactory samples . . . by which it may be judged that in a short time large profit may be derived.

Questions

1. Explain why, in Source F, Venice was the ultimate destination for the spices. (2 marks)
2. How accurate is Source G in claiming for Spain in 1496 the domination of 'a large part of Italy and the Isles of the Mediterranean Sea'? (4 marks)
3. Do these sources provide a complete explanation of the motives for Spanish involvement in the voyages of exploration? (5 marks)

4. What were the terms of the papal donation of 1493? Is it true to say that this grant was biased in favour of Spain? (6 marks)
*5. To what extent do these sources indicate that the good opinion of other powers was an important element in the conduct of foreign policy? (8 marks)

Worked answer

*5. *[It is reasonable to point out that these sources concern only one limited aspect of the foreign policy of Ferdinand and Isabella; but the main thrust of your answer should be to the point, looking at each source in turn before reaching a conclusion.]*

Because the trade with the East was, by the fifteenth century, so important to Europe, the voyages of exploration were bound to influence and be influenced by other aspects of foreign policy. Source F suggests that the Portuguese were revelling in their success, and in fact the Catholic monarchs were to respond with similar gloating messages about their successes in the New World. Status was clearly more important in the long struggle with Portugal than good opinion. Antonio de Nebrija is more concerned with impressing his employers than with accuracy. It is an overstatement to suggest that the war had been carried to North Africa, and it was becoming clear by 1496 that the New World had nothing to do with the Indies. The overstatement of the holdings of Aragon is combined with an implied insult to the Holy Roman Emperor. This is surprising at a time of ongoing negotiations about marriage links with the Habsburgs. Source H suggests that the monarchs were determined to enjoy their new possessions without opposition, but the papal Bull *Inter Cetera* had the effect of upsetting several rulers of Europe, notably the Kings of France, while it did nothing to safeguard Spanish holdings against encroachment by Portugal and by other powers as the sixteenth century got under way. Sources H and I indicate that the monarchs were intent on glory, in particular the glory which would be provided by enhanced wealth.

Many aspects of Ferdinand's foreign policy had little to do with the voyages of exploration. Although the rivalry with Portugal was fought out in oceanic voyages, the more costly disputes with France were concerned with territory in Europe, and there the only criterion was success. On several occasions treaty terms were broken or ignored, and the good opinion of other powers was less important than their respect. As we have seen, Machiavelli found Ferdinand's determined and ruthless approach admirable and effective.

4

CHARLES I AS RULER OF SPAIN

BACKGROUND NARRATIVE

When Ferdinand died, in February 1516, Charles was in his duchy of Burgundy, of which he had been ruler since his father's death in 1506. He did not arrive in Spain until the September of 1517. In the interval, Archbishop Ximenez de Cisneros held his throne secure for him: but there were many who wanted Charles' brother Ferdinand, Spanish by upbringing, and with no ties elsewhere, to take the throne. It is ironic that, in the event, Ferdinand was to become ruler of the Habsburg lands in Germany, and leave Castile. Charles made a poor impression when he arrived, with his protruding Habsburg jaw, surrounded by his Flemish courtiers, and unable to speak Castilian. The Cortes of Castile, meeting at Toledo showed extreme reluctance to hand over full power to this young representative of a foreign dynasty. In the event, equally suspicious of Ferdinand, they declared Charles and his mother Joanna to be joint-sovereigns. In practice the Queen was kept secluded in Tordesillas – perhaps with good reason, considering her unstable temperament – for the rest of her life, which lasted almost as long as her son's reign.

Charles left Spain in May 1520, following the death of his grandfather Maximilian, in order to ensure his election as Holy Roman Emperor (as Charles V) and did not return until the summer of 1522. His absence was marked by the Revolt of the *Comuñeros*, a rising of townspeople with long-standing grievances exacerbated by the departure of the King. Only with difficulty did royal troops eventually suppress the rebellion, but Charles found Spain at peace on his return. The next seven years were to be spent based in Spain, perhaps because Charles had recognised that the *comuñeros'* grievances must be addressed. During these years he married Isabella of Portugal. This marriage, and the birth of his son and heir in May 1527, pleased his Spanish subjects. In his subsequent absences from Spain, his wife and then his son Philip were to act as regents, strengthening the personal ties between the Emperor and his Iberian kingdoms. And Charles was to be absent for most of the rest of his reign. Between 1529 and 1556, the cumulative total of his time in Spain was six years, mostly in brief visits of 12–18 months.

Although Charles visited each of his European lands in turn, it was out of the question that he would visit his largest and newest possessions. The New World was being opened up to Spanish influence at a rapid rate. In the early 1520s, Mexico was conquered by Hernán Cortés and his followers, and during the next decade a tiny handful of Spaniards, under the unsavoury Francisco Pizarro brought the mountain empire of Peru (which included modern-day Bolivia, Ecuador and Chile) into Charles' empire. These new holdings brought new wealth and trading opportunities, but also additional issues of government. The concerns, first expressed by Isabella, about the treatment of the native peoples became more and more acute as their populations declined; and, at the same time, the *conquistadores* appeared to be becoming the same kind of semi-autonomous and arrogant fighting nobility as had plagued Spain in the centuries of the *reconquista*, when they made and unmade monarchs almost at will. Wherever Charles was, he kept in touch with his Council of the Indies, and worked on policies which would solve these twin problems.

Charles' absences, after the first, did not mean that Spain was poorly governed. Charles built upon the work of his grandparents, and put in place mechanisms to ensure that royal control was exercised even when he was not there. Aragon, of course, was used to absentee rulers, and the system of councils which Ferdinand had employed was now applied throughout Iberia. The Council of Castile continued to deal with judicial matters, the Council of Finance with revenue, and the Council of State with general policy. A new council was established in 1524, to supervise the Indies. Following the hostility to his Flemish advisers demonstrated by the *comuñeros*, Charles took care to make use of Spanish ministers. The sense of his absence was diminished, as Brandi made clear in his great biography of Charles, by the use of family members, and by detailed consultation.[1] The nobles remained loyal, in part because they had been much alarmed by the radical challenges to their own power that was implicit in the rising of the *comuñeros*, but also because they were bound to the government by their increasing reliance on the income from their *juros* or annuities. Although they had lost much of their power in government through the reforms of Ferdinand and Isabella, they still enjoyed sinecure posts, and the benefits in the form of tax exemptions and other privileges were enough to attract prosperous commoners to the purchase of *hidalguía* (nobility).

It was not only in government that Charles continued the policies of the Catholic monarchs. In 1525, Charles ordered the conversion of all Muslims of Spain and the deportation of those who refused to convert. If the expulsion of the Jews in 1492 had harmed Spain's commerce, this further Christianisation, though only half-heartedly imposed on this occasion, removed from Spain experts in irrigation and the types of farming appropriate to the arid south. The next few decades would see a strengthening of the concept of *limpieza de san,;re*. The belief grew that only those of 'pure blood' could be entirely relied upon, and so the Jewish and Islamic families who had converted found themselves barred from a growing number of offices and social positions. At the same time, the Holy Office of the Inquisition was encouraged to continue its work of maintaining the spiritual purity of Spain. Concerned about the development of heresy, the Inquisition was able not only to keep Lutheranism at bay but to call into question the fashionable Erasmianism of the court. Excessive piety was also seen as suspect, and, for example, Ignatius Loyola, who was later to set up the Society of Jesus, was questioned on two occasions, in 1526 and 1527.

Ferdinand and Isabella had made use of revenues from the Church; Charles, with his much greater financial commitments, also found these incomes essential. The *Tercia Real* continued to be collected, as did the *subsidio* levy on all clerical rents and incomes. Thanks to the work of his grandparents, Charles also controlled the revenues of the military religious orders, and of vacant dioceses. Despite the fact that the conquest of Granada was a generation in the past, Charles continued to collect the cruzada: the income from the crusading indulgences. Over the whole of his reign, these averaged an annual sale of 7,000.

Wealth not available to Charles' predecessors was arriving in increasing amounts from the Indies. The crown was entitled to the *Quinto Real*, a fifth of all revenues from the New World, and in addition owned many of the sources of gold and silver. Some of the treasure was available only once. The ransom paid by the Incas to free their imprisoned Emperor Atahuallpa was enormous, and it was said that nine forges were engaged for a whole month merely to melt it into bars. Calculations derived from J. Alden Mason[2] and S. K. Lothrop[3] suggest that the total amount, in modern terms, could have been as much as £1.67 billion, of which one-fifth belonged to the crown. Indeed, if we add in gifts, confiscations and taxation payments, it is probable that over 40 per cent of the bullion arriving in Spain was the property of the Emperor. It is therefore all the more remarkable that Charles was forced to call the Cortes on a regular basis, and to request *servicio* taxes from them. During Charles' reign the amount collected quadrupled, even though the percentage of the population exempt from taxation was increasing all the time. In addition, the government collected the *alcabalá*, or sales tax, and the *montazgo* on the movement of sheep. Yet so vast were Charles' commitments as Holy Roman Emperor and dynastic ruler of much of Western Europe, that he was often obliged to borrow substantial amounts, not only from his own people with the issue of *juros*, but extensively from banks in Germany.

The economy of Spain was being affected by three main factors. First, the *juros* appear to have encouraged the prosperous to acquire the status and leisured lifestyle of the *hidalguía*. Second, the balance between wool and grain production continued to be distorted by the *Mesta*, and by the growth in population, which in turn made the importation of grain essential. Above all, the impact of the Spanish empire in America had the effect of further stimulating the production of wool for export, while at the same time pulling people into the towns, notably Seville. The burdens of taxation and the shortage of cereals were to affect the everyday life of the Spanish peasants far more than would the glory of a great empire abroad.

Although Charles had spent so much of his life outside Spain, he resolved to spend his last years there. His abdication in 1556 was followed by two years of retired life in the monastery at Yuste, where he prepared to meet his Maker. The months before his abdication had been filled with negotiations, discussions and papers as decisions were made which would ensure that no future monarch ever had the same territorial possessions, and problems, as Charles. From 1543 onwards, Prince Philip had been regent in Spain during the absences of his father, assisted by such loyal servants of the crown as Francisco de los Cobos, who had been prominent in administration as secretary to several of the government councils. The premature deaths of Charles' other legitimate sons meant that there would be no division of the empire between Philip and his brothers. Instead, Charles determined to detach some of his lands and give them to *his* brother Ferdinand and his descendants. Spain, together with the Netherlands and his holdings in Italy, and, of course the New World, were to be ruled by Philip. The handover was completed in 1556, and Charles, until his death in November 1558, played no further part in government. He left to his son a country with growing economic and financial problems, and whose people were determined that their ruler should concentrate on them alone. The analyses which follow consider Charles' policies and problems in these two areas.

ANALYSIS (1): HOW FAR IS IT TRUE TO SAY THAT CHARLES V NEGLECTED HIS SPANISH POSSESSIONS?

By the most direct measure, that of his actual presence, Charles must be said to have neglected his Spanish lands. Of the forty years of his reign only fifteen-and-a-half were spent in Spain, and the only lengthy period was that following the Revolt of the *Comuñeros*, who had certainly felt that he was neglecting his responsibilities.

When, on 30 May 1520, a mob invaded Segovia City Council, dragged out Rodrigo de Tordesillas, who had represented the city at the Cortes of Santiago earlier that year, and hanged him, one of their complaints was the departure of the King. Once the *Junta* of the Towns was formed, the Articles which they put together at Valladolid also demanded that the King should appoint only Spanish advisers and officials. Historians ever since have accepted that the departure of the King was the precipitant for this rising; there were, however, other factors, and the townsmen may have risen against the government even without the King's 'neglect'. Stephen Haliczer[4] summarises the different views of historians from the sixteenth century onwards. During the nineteenth century, contemporary debates about the State as a mechanism for progress cast the *comuñeros* as dangerous reactionaries; Marxist historians, such as Joseph Peréz in 1970, suggested that the urban bourgeoisie were attempting to replace the aristocrats. Haliczer himself makes the point that the weak government of the last years of Ferdinand had resulted in renewed benefits for the nobility, at the expense of the previously favoured townspeople. Henry Kamen, too, has pointed to the indignation expressed by Castilians that Charles should have spent so much of his brief visit in Aragon rather than among them.[5] All kinds of other permutations of economic, constitutional and nationalistic motives have been suggested; however, the demands of the *junta* made clear that the King's neglect was one of its key grievances.

Following the eventual defeat of the *comuñeros* at the Battle of Villalar on 23 April 1521, Charles in fact implemented a large number of the Articles of the Junta.

Another symptom of Charles' neglect of his Spanish inheritance can be seen in his early personal behaviour: the time it took him to arrive after his grandfather's death was hardly calculated to placate his Iberian subjects; an inability to speak any of the languages of the peninsula might be excused in an ordinary foreigner aged 17, but Charles, and indeed his tutors, had known of his rights and likely inheritance since the death of his father, Philip I, and the consequent mental breakdown of his mother. Charles was aware of the consequences of this mistake and, to his credit, later strove to amend it, acquiring workable Castilian and even some Catalan – the last Spanish King to do so until Juan Carlos I, who became King in 1975. The fact that he was able subsequently to acquire some competence in both Castilian and Catalan, made his initial inability to speak the language of his subjects seem insulting. In addition, his treatment of Cardinal Ximenez de Cisneros was cold and unfeeling. It was the Cardinal who had protected his interests until his arrival, and ensured that his brother was not chosen by the Cortes; and yet the old man was dismissed by letter, and many in Spain believed that his death was caused by a 'broken heart'. This kind of contemptuous behaviour did not endear Charles to the Spanish.

In these early months, Charles' main interest in Spain appeared to be the amount of money which could be raised to assist his other imperial territories and ambitions. It was, after all, the Cortes at Santiago which had sparked the trouble at Segovia. The *comuñeros* demanded that in future meetings of the Cortes the hearing of grievances should always precede fiscal debates. Throughout his reign, the chauvinistic perception that Charles was raising revenues in Spain only to spend them uselessly abroad was never far away.

Seen through Charles' eyes, however, these early issues of the reign take on a different focus. All areas of his empire were important to Charles, and the increase of territory and status abroad brought glory to Spain. It is hard to imagine the Spanish being pleased if their enemy, the King of France, had become Holy Roman Emperor. Charles left Spain in the hands of the man he trusted most, Adrian of Utrecht, without apparently noticing that this was unacceptable to the Spanish: by making Adrian a Spanish citizen, he felt he had overcome the main obstacle, and he was certain of his loyalty. Once he realised that Spanish xenophobia was a serious issue, he found other regents, and made use of the members of his family, to ensure a royal presence when he was away, just as he did in other parts of his empire. His Portuguese wife was, in all his absences until her death, a popular and successful regent. Subsequently, his son, with careful guidance, became regent. The letters and advice which flowed between Spain and Charles, wherever he was, show that the government was his. Given that Charles was not going to relinquish his non-Spanish lands, the government of Spain was as personal as he could make it. Only in Castile was the constant presence of the monarch the norm: the provinces of Aragon had been used to absent leadership, and Ferdinand and Isabella had established a system which could work well in the absence of the King. The councils which controlled the various aspects of the administration functioned competently. Charles was always in touch, by courier and mail, and many decisions were made by him, even when this led to undesirable delays. The Spanish lands in America were of particular interest to him, and he saw all the papers of the Council of the Indies. The decision to appoint a Viceroy for New Spain, in 1530, was an attempt to deal with the ambitions of Hernán Cortés, and Charles was closely concerned with both the choice of Antonio Mendoza, and with the selection of the preliminary *audiencia* which went to consider the situation before the Viceroy's arrival in 1535. He was also involved in the intellectual debates, at the University of Salamanca, about the ethical basis of empire.

His concern for his subjects' well-being was also evident in the spiritual care he exercised over his people. During the 1530s, he ordered the expulsion of converted Jews, on the grounds that their conversions were insecure. To a modern eye, this appears as unwarranted persecution, but in the context of the sixteenth century, it was designed to save souls. At the same time, Charles' failure to suppress the heresy of Martin Luther in Germany made him the more determined to prevent the spread of Protestantism in his other lands. In Spain, the Universities were 'purged' of Erasmian scholars, lest their critiques of the Church should lead to more serious threats to the salvation of Spanish souls. His son, as he grew to adulthood, was a true Christian ruler, and was present except during his marital expedition to England 1554–55. The King was present through his representative, and Castile learned to accept that, just as Aragon had done for centuries.

Of course, many of the problems of Spain were not amenable to solution, even had the King himself been constantly there: issues of finance and inflation, of the economy, of migration and urbanisation, of the wool and cloth trades, which are discussed later in this chapter, continued to exist, wherever the King might be, although some of his policies increased the financial and fiscal difficulties of the peninsula. But Charles, like other contemporary rulers, felt that his wars were just wars, waged not only for the honour of his dynasty, but also for the physical and spiritual benefit of his people. Thus he did not perceive his frequent absences as damaging.

Charles' commitment to Spain was borne out by the fact that there was no serious rebellion in the peninsula after 1521. His presence for seven years was helpful, but after that, he was able to make only brief visits. These were years of war, and of very high taxation, much of which was spent in other parts of the empire. Charles was always inclined to tax the more compliant of his realms: at the start of his reign, it had been the Netherlands which had borne the brunt of his costs: but following risings in Ghent, he moved his main attentions to Spain: a clear indication of his confidence that Spain felt loyal, and had overcome its anger at his early neglect.

Questions

1. Account for Charles V's initial difficulties and eventual success in the government of his Spanish kingdoms. (UCLES Summer 1998)
2. Consider the judgement that during the reign of Charles I the government of Spain and its overseas empire was grossly inefficient. (AEB Summer 1998)

ANALYSIS (2): WHAT FINANCIAL AND ECONOMIC PROBLEMS AFFECTED SPAIN DURING THE REIGN OF CHARLES I?

None of the financial and economic problems which beset Spain during the first half of the sixteenth century was caused by Charles. Few were unique to Spain, many had existed before he came to the throne, and all were to continue and worsen during the reign of his son. On the other hand, Charles' expenditure on foreign policies was greater even than

Ferdinand's had been, and his easy access to German bankers prepared to lend money made his inherited problems more acute.

Following the defeat of the *comuñeros*, there was very little opposition to taxation in Spain. The triple Cortes in Aragon voted money when asked, as did Castile's. All the taxes, and the Church revenues, on which Ferdinand and Isabella had relied, were available to Charles. During the 1530s, Aragon provided about 200,000 ducats per year. To put this into context, however, we need to note that the kingdom of Naples produced 290,000 ducats and the duchy of Milan 300,000. In Castile, the *alcabalá* (sales tax) alone raised 267,000 ducats.[6] In theory, the increasing population should have made possible a reduction in taxation per head. In fact, the increasing frequency with which the *servicio* was levied, and the rising amounts demanded meant that the tax burden went up. Misuse of power by the Cortes members (*procuradores*) was also seen in their ability to shift the burden of taxation away from the towns they represented to the surrounding rural areas (*partidos*) over which they exercised administrative control. Indeed, without this taxation, the instalments of their *juro* annuities would not be paid.

When new taxes were suggested however, they were not so easily accepted, as landowners recognised that their incomes would be adversely affected by even higher levels of taxation on their tenants. Thus the *sisa*, or tax on foodstuff, put forward in 1538, was firmly turned down. Even without this tax, Charles' Spanish income was approximately 1 million ducats a year. But it was impossible for his government to manage on this amount, not least because of the inflation which beset Spain as well as the rest of Europe. Where total crown income probably increased by 50 per cent, prices more than doubled. During his reign, Charles I borrowed a total of 39 million ducats. Some of this was borrowed from his own subjects, by the issue of *juros*: annuities paying 7 per cent per year. Of course, these only made his revenue problems worse: by 1543, more than 65 per cent of Cortes revenue was used in paying out on the *juros*; but at the same time, they ensured the loyalty of the nobility, who were the main recipients. Far greater amounts were borrowed from bankers in Germany, whose initial willingness, however, soon changed to a reluctance, as reflected in their ever-higher interest rates. In an attempt to convince them of the security of their investments, the crown used the method of the *asiento*: this was an agreement, including in the initial borrowing contract, specifying which sources of income would go to service and eventually pay off the debt.

It is not surprising that the German bankers were willing to lend to Charles, since it seemed that untold wealth was pouring into his treasury from his lands in America. While it is hard to find precise figures for the reign of Charles alone, it is clear that the total amount of silver in Europe trebled between 1503 and 1660, the period over the course of which 16 million kilograms of silver arrived in Castile. The huge influx began towards the end of Charles' reign, once the great Potosí mines became workable in the 1550s; but as it was preceded in the 1530s by the gold arriving after the payment of the ransom for the Inca leader Atahuallpa, it is not surprising that the rest of Europe should have been dazzled by the glitter. And much of this bullion was the King's, possibly as much as 40 per cent. In addition to the output of the royal mines, there was the *Quinto Real* and the *almojarifazgo* duty of 7.5 per cent on all imperial goods. Measures to control this trade had been put in place by Isabella, who had reserved the trade to Castilians only (1501) and ensured that all trade was routed through the *Casa de Contratacion* in Seville (1503). Although in 1524 foreign traders were allowed to participate – and from 1525–26 agreements were made permitting any of the emperor's subjects to trade – the Spanish monopoly was restored in 1538. Of all the bullion leaving America, at least 40 per cent did not land in Spain, being immediately forwarded to Germany to service the King's debts.

Inflation made all the King's financial problems more acute. In his 1556 lectures at Salamanca University, Azpilcueta suggested that the appalling rise in commodity prices was being caused by bullion imports. However, it is clear that the causes of inflation were both more deep-rooted and more universal. Spain was one of the few countries in Europe not to have to debase its coinage as a reaction to rising prices, and the wisdom of the period was that bad quality money in itself was a cause of inflation. A rising population and a shortage of commodities were as much causes of inflation as the influx of precious metals. James Casey, in his *Social History of Early Modern Spain*, puts the contemporary theories into the context of more modern scholarship.[7]

The King's financial problems were a symptom, rather than a cause, of the underlying economic difficulties of Spain. A rising population is not necessarily a reason for economic concern: indeed, the wars of the sixteenth century made rulers regard the growing numbers of their citizens with pleasure. But in Spain, rapid population increase put all kinds of pressures on the economy. Within the limitations of pre-census accuracy, it seems likely that the population of Spain was in the region of 4.7 million in 1534, rising to 6.7 million by 1591.[8] This population rise was not, however, evenly spread. Some parts of Spain were unable to sustain a large population; in addition, the towns were exercising a magnetic pull. The population of Seville, for example, went from 60,000 (1500) to 150,000 (1588). The peasant farmers of Castile could not supply sufficient grain for the whole population, and so grain imports increased throughout the reign. These came in the main from Calibre, in south Italy, and therefore the threat from North African pirates was one which the King could not ignore. It was a measure of the problems with wheat production that maize, Indian corn, was to become an important staple in Spain.

The demand for grain might have been expected to increase the amount of arable production in Spain, but the reverse was the case. The powerful sheep production guild, the *Mesta*, making, as it did, substantial payments to the crown, was able to safeguard and even increase its share of the land during the reign of Charles. There were an estimated 3 million *Mesta* sheep in Spain at the start of Charles reign, migrating across protected sheep walks to be sheared near the textile manufacturing areas (e.g. Seville) and back to the northern pastures for grazing in the dry season. In addition, Spain had perhaps 12 million *estantes* (non-migratory sheep).[9] Shortage of bread was bound to push up the prices of all commodities. But there was also, by the end of Charles' reign, a serious shortage of other essential commodities. Over three-quarters of Spain's textile production was going abroad, much of it to New Spain. While in Peru there were yarn-bearing animals, the vicuna and llama, in Mexico there were no large herbivores at all until they were brought in by the Spanish. As a result, the demand for textiles was insatiable, and traders were happy to exchange woollen cloth for bullion.

Spain was, at the same time, losing a proportion of its most entrepreneurial subjects. Following the forced expulsions of the productive Jewish and Muslim populations, the voluntary emigration to the New World attracted many of the more enterprising citizens of Castile. In Peru, for instance, it was possible for an artisan from Estremadura to become a gentleman: a blacksmith was granted an *encomienda* near Quito in 1536. The shortage of textile producers in Spain can be identified from government regulations: between 1548 and 1552 there was an attempt to ban all exports of textiles, except to the Indies, to ensure adequate supplies. Even more damaging, in the long run, was the fact that Flemish and French textiles were seen as of a higher quality than the domestic product: thus, despite heavy demand, the Spanish textile industry declined in the face of competition from abroad, exacerbating the shortage of commodities, and therefore the inflation.

The emphasis on the trade with the Indies caused other economic problems for Spain. A shortage of wood for ship building meant that it was necessary to build ships in the north, away from Seville and Cadiz, and also to trade with the Baltic lands. The shortage of wood, which already meant that peasants had problems finding fuel for warmth and cooking, reduced the number of new ships that the Spanish could build.

Their solution was to build fewer but bigger, and more seaworthy, ships. This policy was to backfire in major losses during the reign of Philip II.

Indeed, many of the financial and economic problems which had beset Charles were to prove disastrous in the reign of his successor. Spain's commitment to the defence of an expanding global empire meant that its financial affairs were always difficult, and budgeting in the modern sense impossible. Imports of the bullion upon which constant borrowing and spending were secured meant that the inflationary spiral which affected all Europe hit Spain first and hardest. Charles had done what seemed to him right both at home and abroad; the underlying weaknesses of the Spanish economy were neither recognisable nor remediable in the context of the sixteenth century.

Questions

1. How justified is the view that Spain and her Empire during the reign of Charles I experienced success in government but financial and economic failure? (AEB Summer 1997)
2. 'The possession of an overseas empire brought more problems than benefits to Spain.' How far do you agree? (EDEXCEL Summer 1998)

SOURCES

1. GOVERNING SPAIN

Source A: a letter from Sir Thomas Spinelly to Cardinal Wolsey, 3 May 1520.

The Estates of Castile have granted to the King, for the continuation of the war, four hundred and fifty thousand ducats, to be paid in three years by even portions, beginning the first payment in January of the year 21, and the same estates have accepted by a common consent for Lieutenant General the Cardinal of Tortosa. ... The Archbishop of Cosence, an Italian ... is also elected Privy Councillor.

Source B: Adrian of Utrecht writes to Charles, September 1520.

There is no way for us to obtain money for the courier post here; the other day we searched for money to send a despatch to Navarre but were unable to find any. Large sums are owed to the master of the post, but nothing can be found to pay him. My salary is not being paid, and I haven't enough of my own to meet such great expenses. I pray that your majesty will give me permission to leave here honestly and in sufficient time so that I don't disgrace your service.

Source C: Charles describes his attitude to the Castilian Cortes in 1525.

Since the procuradores of the Cortes, who came at our command, are trying to serve us and to benefit our kingdoms, we are obliged to hear them benevolently and to receive their petitions, both general and special, and to answer them and do them justice; and we are ready to do this as our royal predecessors ordained; and we order that, before the Cortes are concluded, all the general and specific articles which may be presented on behalf of the kingdom shall be answered and that the necessary measures shall be taken as befits our service and the common benefit of our kingdoms.

Source D: Charles gives advice to his son Philip, newly appointed regent in Spain, 1542.

To enable you the better to fulfil your part, I have left you here in Spain all the members of my Royal Council and given special instructions to them, which I send to you with Cobos. I beseech you to act in accordance with what I tell you. The Royal Council will see to the administration of Justice, and will care for the welfare of the land. Support them in their endeavours. Do not permit the publication of interdicts and the prohibition of worship, except on the most urgent grounds, or unless the commands proceed from the Holy See, when you must religiously respect them, for in these times many men no longer respect the Holy See. Trust the Duke of Alba as commander-in-chief of the army, obey my instructions in your dealings with the Council of State, the Councils for the Indies, for Finance, for the Order of the Golden Fleece and in your relations with the Inquisition. Have a special care to finance which is today the most important department of State. The Treasury has a clear knowledge of the means which are at your disposal . . .

Source E: letter to Charles from Francisco de los Cobos, 1546.

Remember the importance of finding a remedy for the relief of these kingdoms, because of the extreme need for otherwise there could not fail to be serious trouble, because the need is so notorious that not only are the natives of the kingdom aware of it and are refusing to take part in any financial transaction, but even foreigners . . . are doing the same thing, because they know there is no source from which payment can be made.

Questions

*1. Who were Adrian of Utrecht (writer of Source B) and the Duke of Alba (Source D)? (4 marks)
2. Why were the problems described in Source B so acute during the year 1520? (2 marks)
3. In the light of Sources A and B, comment on the relationship between Charles and the Cortes of Castile. (5 marks)
4. How complete a picture can be gained from these sources about the financial situation in Spain during the reign of Charles I? (6 marks)
5. Using these sources and your own knowledge, discuss the extent to which Charles' absences were a problem for the government of Spain. (8 marks)

Worked answer

*1. [While this is just a simple identification question, the allocation of an additional mark suggests that you might add a little more than the basic information.]

Adrian of Utrecht had been Charles' tutor since 1507, and was appointed regent in Spain, to the annoyance of native Spaniards. He was to become Pope (Adrian VI) in 1522.

Fernando Alvarez de Toledo, Duke of Alba, was one of the leading soldiers of his age, and had led the imperial troops in Italy. In the next reign, he was to be appointed to quell the rebellion in the Netherlands.

2. THE REVOLT OF THE *COMUÑEROS*

Source F: the Council of Segovia warns Cisneros of what might happen if Charles does not return to Spain (1517).

[These] Kingdoms would be justified in trying other means and in such case those that are now declared to be unlawful and dishonest would become appropriate and it would not appear unreasonable for such noble cities and so courageous a people to demand whatever they feel is for the good of these Kingdoms.

Source G: a letter to Cardinal Wolsey, from Thomas Spinelly, 27 June 1520.

A rumour is spread of a commotion in Spain. By letters from Valladolid on the 14th, the Cardinal of Tortosa advises that, at the return home of the deputies of

Segovia . . . the commons insurrexed against them, crying *Viva el Rey et mora el mal conseyo*, accusing them of granting money unto the king without securing the articles to be demanded of them. . . . The seventeen cities and towns require (1) that the alcabalá, the principal rent of the crown, should be given in farm to the cities that pay it . . . (2) that benefices be not given to strangers; (3) that gold and silver be not sent out of the realm; (4) that processes be not deferred.

Source H: the Revolt of the *Comuñeros*, 1520, described by a contemporary.

The communes of Castile began their revolt, but after a good start had a bad ending and exalted beyond what it had previously been the power of the King, whom they desired to abase. They rose in revolt because the King was leaving the realm, because of the *servicio*, because of the foreign regent, because of the large amounts of money which were being taken out of the realm, and because the chief office of the treasury had been given to Chievres, the archbishopric of Toledo to William de Croy, and knighthoods of the military orders to foreigners . . .

Source I: news out of Spain – a letter to England from Valladolid, dated 2 September 1520.

John de Padilla was at Tordesillas in constant communication with the estates at Avila and with the Queen, who either will not speak, or not to any purpose. The estates demand an account of the 5,600,000 ducats of gold found by them and of the money received by the Emperor since the decease of the King of Aragon; that the farm of the crown revenues be given to the towns and not to the *marrans*; that appointments be given to subjects, not strangers. . . . The commons of Seville have broken open the prisons of the Inquisition and delivered the prisoners. The Emperor's portion of the gold of the Indies has been seized by the commons for the use of the towns. The tithes of the Archbishop have been refused. There is no other remedy, except the immediate return of the Emperor to Spain.

Source J: Charles explains to the Castilian Council of State why he is going to Italy (November 1528).

The purpose of my going to Italy is to work with the Pope for a general Council of the Church, to be held either in Italy or in Germany, which will wipe out heresies and bring about the reform of the Church. . . . And in the next world I would by God's judgement have to suffer much if I did not do all in my power and venture all I have to reform the Church and wipe out this abominable heresy. It is also my aim in going to Italy to sort out, calm down, and pacify that land where, as you have heard and know, for eight full years my armies have suffered immeasurably.

I can discharge my obligations and afford recompense in no better way than by putting an end to the long running war and securing a permanent and genuine peace. It is as much my intention in going to Italy to see my kingdoms and lands and the subjects who dwell within them. . . . However well or justly our vassals may be governed, there must be some whose conditions may be improved or who are aggrieved in some way.

Questions

1. Who were Juan de Padilla and 'the Queen' (Source I)? (2 marks)
*2. Why would English observers (Sources G and I) be interested in these events in Spain? (4 marks)
3. How complete a picture can be obtained from these sources of the demands of the *comuñeros*? (6 marks)
4. Consider the content and tone of Source J. How convincing do you think this statement would have been to the wider public of Castile? (6 marks)
5. From your knowledge of the reign of Charles I, and with reference to these sources, discuss the extent to which the government of Spain was changed by the rebellion and its defeat (7 marks)

Worked answer

*2. *[Note that one of these sources is a 'government' reporter, while the other appears to be a private individual; make sure that you make use of any knowledge you have of other aspects of the period.]*

All the powers of Europe were interested in events within the huge holdings of Charles V, particularly after the convoluted negotiations of the imperial elections. Henry VIII had been discussing an alliance with Charles V to maintain the relationship established with Ferdinand. But Henry was also negotiating with Francis I (the discussions which were to culminate at the Field of the Cloth of Gold, 1521). Thus anything that affected the status and power of Charles at home would have been of interest, and Wolsey would have been keen that his ambassadors provided all the information they could. In addition, the threat of civil disorder was a reality in all the states of Europe; Henry VII had survived several major rebellions, although his son had not yet met serious opposition. Thus a kind of envious relish may have encouraged travellers of all kinds to describe and comment on the domestic problems of Spain.

5

FOREIGN AFFAIRS DURING THE REIGN OF CHARLES I

BACKGROUND NARRATIVE

Charles I's inheritance ensured that he would need to spend much time, money and effort on issues outside Spain. As Ferdinand's heir, he confronted France, both in the Pyrenees and in Italy. His duchy of Burgundy included lands which were claimed by France and conversely, as Duke, he needed to repossess the provinces which France had taken over. As heir to Maximilian von Habsburg, the lands of south-eastern Europe were his concern and, once elected Holy Roman Emperor in 1519, the states of Germany became his responsibility too. As far as the Spanish were concerned, time spent ruling his other kingdoms was time spent on and in foreign lands; but, for Charles, all parts of his empire were equally his, and while he never strove to unite them he nevertheless treated them all as part of a family of which he was the head.

Relations with Portugal were much more settled than they had been during the reigns of the Catholic monarchs. The marriage of Isabella to Charles led to fifty settled years, during which rivalries were played out in the Atlantic and the Americas, rather than on the Iberian peninsula. John III (1521–57) married Charles' sister Catherine and was persuaded to adopt the same religious policies as Spain, and to expel his Jews and Muslims. By the end of Charles' reign it had become clear that the death of John's son, which left his infant grandson heir to the throne of Portugal, would provide new opportunities for a Castilian takeover.

The war against France lasted throughout Charles' reign, draining Spanish resources and manpower. Although Chièvres had tried to ensure friendship, he could not overcome the many causes for hostility between France and the Habsburg Emperor. In 1521 French attacks on Navarre and Luxembourg ended the brief period of peace which had followed the 1516 Treaty of Noyon, and enabled Charles to gain and keep Tournai. Charles' Holy League now repossessed Milan, inviting a French counter-attack. The fighting in Italy ended in a triumphant victory for Charles, at the Battle of Pavia (1525). The Treaty of Madrid, which the captured Francis I signed, appeared to settle many of the outstanding conflicts, since Francis gave up his claims to Flanders, Burgundy, Artois, Milan and Naples. His two sons were to be hostages until the Treaty's terms were fulfilled, and he was to marry Charles' sister Eleanor.

His repudiation of the Treaty as having been signed under duress came less than six months later. Francis' attempts to justify his actions – 'how many times did I not warn him that it was not in my power to dismember the Kingdom?'[1] – did not reduce the anger felt by Charles and demonstrated on the two young French princes: they remained in prison in Spain for three years. The fighting in Italy continued, its worst point being the sack of Rome in 1527 by unpaid imperial troops, until the Treaty of Cambrai was signed in 1529. While Francis' promise to return Burgundy at some future date was unlikely to be fulfilled, the huge ransom for the princes was paid and they were released. Renewed fighting in the 1530s and 1540s was punctuated by the Truce of Nice (1538) and the Treaty of Crepi (1544), but the question of the Burgundian lands remained unsolved, and affected other areas of Charles' concern, as the French made alliances with the Turks and with the Protestant rulers of Germany. Not until after Charles' abdication was any permanent settlement made.

Charles had many reasons to be concerned about the growth in Turkish power, even before the Turks allied with his enemy, the 'Most Christian King of France'. Under the Emperor Suleiman (1520–66) the Turks were extending their power both along the Danube and in the Mediterranean, where they captured Rhodes in 1522. The Habsburg hereditary lands in Austria were under threat from the Turkish advance, and Charles' vassal and brother-in-law Lewis of

Hungary died at the Battle of Mohacs in 1526. Vienna itself was besieged in 1529, but supply problems forced the Turkish withdrawal. At the same time, Charles, as ruler of Spain and Naples, was concerned about the depredations of the Moorish pirates under Barbarossa and Dragut Rais. Corn supplies to Spain were threatened, as was the security of all shipping in the western Mediterranean. Charles' expeditions to capture Oran and Tunis were sensational successes, but an even more ambitious attempt on Algiers in 1541 ended in disaster. Francis I's agreement with the Turks in 1543, allowing them to use Toulon as a naval base against Spain, was a further blow to the security of Charles' possessions in southern Europe.

Francis also used Charles' problems in Germany as a weapon against him. The title of Holy Roman Emperor had little meaning in terms of government; Charles' grandfather had failed to impose a 'common penny' tax, and most of the Princes in Germany preferred to ignore the imperial authority. Having spent so much on his election, Charles found little reward in Germany, and appointed his brother as regent in 1522, leaving to him the everyday government of the empire and the Habsburg lands. But by 1522, the course of events in Germany had already been set. The protest of Martin Luther had initially been dealt with by Charles in a truly Renaissance manner: a Diet had been called at Worms (1521), with the different sides of the argument brought into the open under safe conduct. When Luther refused to recant, however, he was outlawed, and survived thanks only to the protection of Frederick, Elector of Saxony. It was at this stage that Charles returned to Spain, and so one might suggest that what followed in Germany was not his fault. Martyn Rady, however, points out that Charles tied his brother's hands by frequently promising to return to Germany, and by failing to provide clear guidance.[2] The German princes seized on the pretext of religious difference to establish their own authority, and by the time Charles did return – to hold a Diet at Augsburg (1530) – the lines of demarcation were set. In 1531, the Protestant princes formed the League of Schmalkalde to protect their interests, getting support from the rulers of Denmark and England as well as France. Direct fighting was avoided, and a further attempt at theological compromise was sought at Regensburg in 1541. But by 1546 it was clear that war could not be avoided, since the Protestant princes rejected the authority of the General Council of the Church, meeting in Trent. The Schmalkaldic war lasted less than a year, ending in a tremendous victory for Charles at Mühlberg (1547), but it solved nothing. The princes would not return to imperial control, and the Protestants would not return to Catholicism, so that fighting continued sporadically, with many princes changing sides as local territorial interests influenced. The settlement finally made at Augsburg in 1555, Charles' last action as Emperor, could have been made twenty years earlier, since it enshrined the principle that religion should be decided by the ruler of each state. Germany and Austria ceased, with Charles' abdication, to have any ties with Spain other than those of marriage and family. Indeed, from Spain's point of view, for much of Charles' reign Germany had been no more than a distraction and an expense.

The Netherlands were a completely different matter. Charles' own home and birthplace, these were also among the richest lands in Europe, controlling the land routes which linked northern Europe to Italy, and dominating the sea trade with the Baltic. In 1531 the Council of Flanders was established, along the lines of the various Councils in Castile and Aragon, and the States General continued to meet, particularly to give consent to taxation. The Netherlands were enlarged by territory gained from France and from the German princes in the north. Personal loyalty to Charles ensured stability even during his long absences, but there were developments hinting at the troubles which were to beset Charles' son in the Netherlands. In 1522, an Inquisition was established, to combat the growth of Lutheranism. The other crisis, which arose in 1539, concerned taxation. The Guilds of Ghent led protests against the heavy taxation being imposed by Charles to fund policies elsewhere. From then on, Charles lightened the tax burden of the Netherlands, at the expense of Spain.

Given the antagonism of his Spanish subjects to anything that took him away from Spain, Charles may be criticised for not abdicating from each of his lands much sooner. But his view of himself as the leader of Christendom, and as the chosen of God, meant that he had to hold on to what he had been given and resist any power which threatened his authority. The two analyses which follow will consider why his war against France lasted so long, and the various motives which impelled him in his handling of foreign issues.

ANALYSIS (1): WHY DID THE HABSBURG–VALOIS STRUGGLE CONTINUE FOR SO LONG?

Any dispute with many causes may be expected to endure for a long time, and the disagreements between Spain and France were already serious before either Charles I or Francis I came to the throne. These disputes were made worse by the personal antipathy between the two men. Francis I had hoped to be Holy Roman Emperor, and was bitter when Charles' bribes and promises proved more effective than his own. His capture at Pavia was a deep humiliation for the French King; his failure to keep his promises forced Charles, in accordance with the diplomatic conventions of the day, to mistreat the two young French princes, sent as hostages in their father's place. When a French courtier visited the princes in 1529, he described their accommodation as

> very dark, without any carpet or decoration save a straw mattress, in the which chamber my Lords were seated on small stone stools beneath a window, barred inside and out . . . and with walls eight or ten feet thick, the said window so high that scarcely could my said Lords have air or the pleasure of daylight.

He was also appalled at the shabbiness of their clothes, and at the fact that three years of captivity had caused them to lose their French.[3] It was not surprising that when the Dauphin Francis died in 1536, the hardships of his captivity were blamed for having weakened his health; nor was it surprising that his brother, as Henry II, King of France, should prove relentless in his loathing of Charles. Peace would not be achieved until both Charles and Francis I were dead.

Because the war had many causes it was fought in many different areas, and thus attempts to achieve peace in one area were likely to fail because of conflicts arising in others. Italy had been the key focus for the earlier wars of Ferdinand; and fighting between Charles and Francis continued over Milan and Naples. Indeed, since many of the mercenaries employed by both sides were Italian, it is not surprising that the war there should be hard fought. But, at the same time, the Spanish possession of the Netherlands widened the theatre of war, with the towns on the eastern border of France being fought over again and again. Francis and his advisers saw the possession of towns such as Cambrai and Tournai to be essential for the maintenance of French security; Charles regarded them as a part of his patrimony. Given, in addition, that the French were reluctant to accept the permanent loss of the Pyrenean provinces, there would always be a new focal point for conflict in one area as soon as the fighting died down in another.

France made this repeated renewal of war more likely by its willingness to become involved in what otherwise may have been seen as Charles' own imperial problems. French support for the Schmalkaldic League undoubtedly extended hostility into the 1540s, as did the Turkish naval base at Toulon. For the French, alliance with Suleiman was a matter of trade as much as of anti-Habsburg policy. The wealth of Asia continued to reach the Mediterranean through the traditional routes of the Persian Gulf and the Red Sea, and France was naturally enthusiastic to take her share. Francis was also more than willing to antagonise Charles by 'trespassing' on his new lands to the west. During the 1520s, the Florentine Giovanni da Verazzano was sponsored to find a route through the New World to the East, regardless of the papal donation of 1493; the marriage of the future Henry II to Catherine de Medici in 1533 was the opportunity to persuade the Medici Pope Clement VII to change the *Inter Cetera* Bull, authorising France also to benefit from the American lands. The journeys of Jacques Cartier, in the 1530s, laid the foundation for the French holdings in Canada. Thus the Habsburg–Valois rivalries of Europe spread to the American continent.

The links between France and the Medici Papacy, and with the Turks, were far from being the only alliances in Europe, and the continual shifting of affinity was in its turn a reason for the continuation of the Habsburg–Valois wars. Henry VIII of England, for example, formed various alliances, and sent troops to participate in the fighting sufficiently frequently to encourage both sides to continue. At the Field of the Cloth of Gold (1520) his friendship with Francis had seemed complete; yet only a month later he was in alliance with Charles, and with the Pope, Leo X. He claimed the French throne in 1522, and fought, albeit unsuccessfully, against Francis in 1523. By 1527, with his hopes for a new wife growing, he abandoned his alliances with Charles, meeting Francis in 1532: indeed, Francis became godfather to the Princess Elizabeth, born the next year. For almost a decade, his marital affairs kept Henry in opposition to Charles: his brief marriage to Anne of Cleves being a reminder of his brief flirtation with the Protestant princes of Germany. By 1543, however, he was again fighting on the Habsburg side, and his armies captured Boulogne in that year. Only Henry's death, in 1547, achieved peace between England and France. While the English involvement had never been definitive, the fact that the support of England might be available was another goad to keep the Habsburg–Valois conflict on its destructive path.

Whatever alliances were signed, a further factor making the continuance of the conflict more likely was the parity of the forces of the two powers. Warfare had, by this time, become a professional and technical business. The kind of army which Ferdinand had developed was by now the norm. Specialist artillery and hand-gun troops were available for hire, and training was regarded as essential for the levied troops which were brought to join them. A war of sieges and convoluted manoeuvres made it virtually impossible to achieve an overwhelming victory. Even the appalling French rout at Pavia brought only a brief intermission in the fighting. The underlying resources were perhaps less balanced. Francis was forced to tax his people savagely. For example, as early as 1529, Francis imposed additional taxes of 40 per cent of revenue from all clergy and all landowners, since by then it was clear that the peasants had no more to give. For Charles, on the other hand, the problem was, in the short term, ameliorated by the bullion arriving from America. The German bankers were willing to lend, since they were assured of repayment with high interest by shiploads of gold and silver. The borrowing and heavy taxation might harm the finances of the two powers, but there was never sufficient resistance to bring the war to an end.

It is possible, however, that had Charles turned his entire attention to the war against France there would have been some kind of conclusion. Throughout his reign, however, he was diverted from one problem to another: after the Revolt of the *Comuñeros*, he needed to spend time in Spain; after the tax rebellions in Ghent, he had to alter the focus of his revenue collection; repeated pleas from his brother in Germany compelled him to visit Germany, however briefly. Thus the Habsburg–Valois war was never more than one of many concerns demanding his attention.

Even the deaths of the main protagonists did not end the war. Admittedly, the new young King of England had regents who realised that the French war was an extravagance they could ill afford: but when Edward VI was replaced by his sister Mary, her Spanish marriage led to a renewed anti-French alliance and, of course, to the loss of Calais. By that time, Francis also was dead, but Henry II's antagonism continued the fighting. Only after Henry's accidental death (1559) had plunged France into a period of religious and civil strife did the Habsburg–Valois struggle end: the factors impelling its continuation had always been much stronger than any wish for peace.

Questions

1. Why was Italy such a persistent concern for Charles V? (UCLES Summer 1998)
2. How far was the hostility between Charles and Francis a personal one?

ANALYSIS (2): WHAT MOTIVES DIRECTED CHARLES I'S FOREIGN POLICIES?

In common with all other princes of this epoch, great and small, Charles believed that God had chosen him to rule his vast inheritance, and that his lands and their peoples were held only in trust on God's behalf. The sequence of marriages and deaths which ensured his vast inheritance seemed to point him towards the dominance of Christendom, and his sense of religious duty was a powerful motivation in his entire reign. His reluctance to give up any of his provinces set him in conflict with his peoples, who each wanted him to concentrate on them. One solution was to use his own family to maintain a personal link with each area.

Charles might never have been elected Holy Roman Emperor. Stewart Macdonald, among others, suggests that the electors recognised the need to elect someone who was in a position to keep the Turks at bay; the Habsburgs were already established in Austria, barring the Danube.[4] In addition, since the electors would obviously prefer neglect to assiduous government, Charles was a better candidate than Francis I precisely because of the former's many other preoccupations. They were right that Charles would not be able to give the empire his full attention. As early as 1522, his brother was put in charge, and was married to Maximilian's daughter, Anne of Austria. Charles did not, however, allow Ferdinand autonomy: instructions and advice flowed across Europe, concerning affairs both in the empire and in the Habsburg family lands. Originally, Charles had promised that Ferdinand would be Emperor after himself, but as the end of his reign approached Charles clearly worried about the dynastic implications of such a division. Not until 1551 was agreement reached between the two branches of the family, and Philip excluded from his father's eastern holdings.

Charles' disappointment at the religious splits within Germany was intense. The agreement finally signed at Augsburg in 1555 could have been signed twenty years earlier, if Charles had been prepared to accept the reality of German religious divisions. His refusal to do so is a measure of another key preoccupation of his foreign policy: his conviction that he was appointed by God to be Defender of the Faith. While he was, within limits, successful in holding back the advance of the Turks into Europe, he was unable to forgive himself for allowing heresy to gain such a firm hold in Germany.

He was determined to ensure that nothing similar occurred in the Netherlands, which were his homelands, his birthplace and his home for the first seventeen years of his life. The varied provinces of The Netherlands had different histories, and in some cases different overlords (for example, as ruler of Flanders and Artois, Charles was nominally the vassal of France) In theory, he ruled them all separately. In practice, from the death of his father his aunt Margaret ruled all the Netherlands as his guardian and regent. Her power was briefly removed when Charles was declared adult in 1514, but she was soon re-established as governor, and remained so in Charles' many absences. When Margaret died, Charles found another member of the family, his widowed sister Mary of Hungary, to take over. Charles' affection for and pride in the Netherlands affected his foreign policy: these were only a part of the historic lands of Burgundy, much of the rest of which had been seized in 1477 by Louis XI of France. Charles believed that it was his destiny to regain the ancestral Burgundian lands. On the other hand, his love of the region made him determined to protect it from heresy. The introduction of a local Inquisition in 1522 may have removed Lutheranism, but its effect was to drive Protestants and Anabaptists into hiding, where they provided a fertile ground for the growth of Calvinism in due course. Nor did his affection for the Netherlands inhibit him when it came to taxing their wealth, leading to rebellion in 1539. Charles worked hard to centralise the provinces of the Low Countries. Succession was made hereditary in 1548, where previously the consent of the Assembly had been, at least nominally, required. It is probable that these centralising mechanisms had the effect of encouraging the provinces to pull together against the Spanish later.

> Under Charles V and even more so under his son Philip II, these lands chafed under what was felt to be, in many respects, a foreign, far-off, uncaring regime. This process of gradual disenchantment with the rulers was accelerated in the latter half of the sixteenth century, when for both the rulers and the ruled the religious controversies between Catholics and Protestants . . . became a focal point in a situation in which the umbilical cord connecting the God-given King and his subjects was already stretched too tautly.[5]

Charles might claim that his wars against France were for the benefit of the Netherlands: they, however, found themselves paying huge amounts in taxes for wars which were being fought on their territory and across their trading routes; thus their markets and, of course, profits were damaged at the same time as their absent Duke was demanding high taxes. When Charles decided to abdicate, he was pleased to be able to maintain the link between Spain and the Netherlands. Nevertheless, the many problems of his reign ensured that the Netherlands would rebel against Spanish rule during the reign of his son.

Just as Charles expected to rule his many lands by using his relatives as regents and governors so, like his grandparents, he relied on marriages to cement alliances. His sisters were married to the Kings of France, Portugal and Hungary, while he and his brother took wives to consolidate relationships with branches of their own families, in Portugal and Austria. Charles' children were married into the royal families of Portugal and England, and his youngest daughter, Mary, married her first cousin, the son of Ferdinand. In these ways, Charles hoped to hold together, even after his abdication, the varied lands which he had himself ruled and fought over.

Charles' perception of his position was defined by his powerful religious faith, and by his determination not to separate what, in the words of the Wedding Mass, God had put together. In the event, this proved impossible, and his rule of his various foreign holdings had to be delegated, as indeed did his rule of the kingdoms of Spain. But it would be an oversimplification to describe his foreign policy as being clearly and directly an expression of his aims. Much of what he did was reactive, as one crisis followed another, and as his allies and enemies shifted their affinities. What would have been best for his lands was probably peace; instead, there was almost continuous war.

The sources which follow offer an opportunity to consider more closely the long years of the Habsburg–Valois conflict, and to examine the problems of government in a far-flung empire.

Questions

1. 'The wonder is not that Charles V achieved so little, but that he achieved anything at all.' Discuss. (UCLES Summer 1997)
2. 'He governed it like the head of a great sixteenth-century merchant house, where the junior members of the family served as heads of the foreign branches of the firm.' Explain and comment upon this (Brandi's) interpretation of Charles V's method of governing his European territories. (UCLES Summer 1998)

SOURCES

1. THE HABSBURG–VALOIS WARS

Source A: Treaty between Charles I and Henry VIII, 25 August 1521.

The contracting parties are to declare themselves open enemies to the King of France in March 1523, and make war upon him by land and sea; the Pope and the Emperor together in Italy for the expulsion of the French before the 15th May of that year.... The King of England likewise shall cross the sea in person before that date and invade France.... The Pope shall, before the ratification of this League, grant dispensations for the marriage between the Emperor and the King of England's daughter Mary, notwithstanding the espousals already made between the Emperor and the French King's daughter and between Mary and the Dauphin ...

Source B: letter from Francis I to Louise, regent of France, February 1524.

Madame. To let you know the extent of my misfortune, nothing remains to me but my honour and my life which are safe. And so that news of me may be of some small comfort to you, I have begged to be allowed to write this letter, which favour has been given to me freely. I beg you not to lose heart, but to employ your usual good sense, for I have confidence that in the end my God will not desert me. I commend unto you my little children, who are also yours, and beg you to hasten the bearer of this on his road to and from Spain – he is on his way to the Emperor to enquire how he wishes me to be treated. And I recommend myself humbly to your kindness.

Source C: letter from Cardinal Campeggio to Cardinal Wolsey, 15 April 1526.

The French King was set free a few days ago. The Imperial Ambassadors are pressing him to ratify the terms; but he answers that he will follow the example of the Emperor, who does nothing of importance without the decision of his Councils, and they must therefore suffer him to go to Paris to hear the opinion of his nobles. For this answer, and because he has left the places where he should have married Leonora, many think he will not keep the compact; and in this, almost all the letters from France agree. Besides, he is diligently fortifying Burgundy, so that it seems certain that, unless some milder terms are agreed on, arms will again be taken up, especially as the Imperialists have occupied the Duchy of Milan.

Source D: report from the Vatican to the papal Nuncio in England, 27 June 1527.

I take the first opportunity of informing you of what has occurred to me since that dreadful day. What Goths, what Vandals, what Turks were ever like this army of the Emperor in the sacrilege they have committed? Volumes would be required to describe but one of their misdeeds. They strewed on the ground the sacred body of Christ, took away the cup, and trod underfoot the relics of the saints to spill their ornaments. No church nor monastery was spared. They violated nuns amid the cries of their mothers, burned the most magnificent buildings, turned churches into stables, made use of crucifixes and other images as marks for their arquebuses. It is no longer Rome, but Rome's grave ...

Source E: letter to a friend in Salamanca, from one of Prince Philip's courtiers, 1554.

The English hate us Spaniards worse than they hate the devil, and treat us accordingly. They rob us in town and on the road. ... This match will be a fine business if the Queen does not have a child, and I myself do not think she will. They were saying in Castile that once His Highness was King of England we would lord it over France, and the very opposite has happened, for the French are stronger than ever, and are gaining ground and burning in Flanders every day. ... They are saying publicly that they intend to see to it in this gathering of theirs that His Highness be not allowed to leave the kingdom without the Queen's and their consent; for they think this realm good enough for its King to be able to do without another. The English being as they are, I should not be at all surprised to see them do it, for they rejoice to see Flanders in the sorry conditions it has found its way into, and would not stir a finger were matters much worse, or even if the Low Countries were lost and the Emperor with them. They are certainly more like Frenchmen than Spaniards.

Questions

1. What was the 'misfortune' (Source B) which had beset Francis I, and on what terms was he 'set free' (Source C)? (2 marks)
2. How do you explain the hostility which (according to Source E) existed between the Spaniards and the English? (4 marks)
*3. Judging by its subject matter and tone, how far would you agree that Source D was designed as propaganda? (5 marks)
4. How much can be learned from these sources about the place of marriage alliances in the field of European diplomacy? (6 marks)
5. To what extent do these sources confirm or refute the suggestion that it was the French who were responsible for the long duration of the wars? (8 marks)

Worked answer

*3. [Although you are not specifically asked to, it is important to show that you know the subject matter of the passage, and to indicate why propaganda might be seen as useful.]

In May 1527, unpaid imperial troops invaded and looted the city of Rome. This was shocking because, although Rome was not in real terms a pure or holy city, nevertheless, the capture of the Pope and the damage done to many religious buildings appalled much of Europe. The Emperor's Chancellery in Castile immediately put out explanations, blaming the Pope for inciting further wars, and the King of France as an oath breaker; thus the Pope needed to respond. The allegiance of Henry VIII was crucial in the alliances of Europe, and the Pope needed to ensure that Charles did not convince Henry into further fighting on the imperial side.

The tone of the letter is one of outrage. Instead of comparing the imperialists only to the current 'worst enemy', the Turks, the Pope also compares them to the Barbarians who destroyed Rome at the end of the Roman empire. Exaggeration is always a mechanism of propaganda: 'no church or monastery was spared'; and specific examples given are designed to shock the readers: the rape of nuns and the destruction of holy relics to seize the jewels of the reliquaries certainly occurred, but attacks were also made on the citizens of Rome, and these are barely mentioned. The assault on the 'sacred body of Christ', or reserved Communion bread, may be designed as a reference to that other attack on the Eucharist, namely the teaching of Martin Luther. If this is the case, the effect is to remind people that the perpetrator of these outrages is the man who has also been letting Luther escape and gather followers in Germany.

2. GOVERNING THE WIDER EMPIRE

Source F: letter of Margaret of Burgundy to Charles of Spain, 9 March 1519.

[There] are two ways by which you may arrange the election in your favour: the first is, by cash ... and the second, Sire, is by force. The French have plainly stated that they will win the Empire by way either of the affection in which Francis is held there, or of money or of force. As regards the last, we are advised that they are preparing on all sides.... The King of France is infiltrating small companies into Italy in order, as rumour has it, to have himself crowned in Rome whether he is elected or not.... Since Francis wishes to employ force, he must be resisted by the same means. We believe, Sire, that you should order a large army to Rosellon and another to Navarre.

Source G: letter of Charles to the Archduke Ferdinand, 25th March 1526.

I advise you to be as conciliatory in dealing with your subjects as possible and wish I could have suggested a plan for dealing with such towns of the Empire as are practising with the princes unfavourable to our interests. . . . I am determined not to meddle nor change anything in our faith or suffer it to receive any injury from the German nation. . . . I have had a letter from the Pope, touching the invasion of Hungary by the Turks. . . . Francis was restored in the 17th; the Princes have been sent to Burgos.

Source H: Charles describes the recapture of Tunis (July 1535).

You know that with our armada we came to Tunis to chase off Barbarossa and the other corsairs, enemies of our Holy Catholic Faith, and to restore King Muley Hassan to the throne, he having requested our help. We took by force the fortress of La Goletta. There the Turks lost nearly everything . . . and many excellent artillery pieces fell into our hands. After occupying La Goletta we marched on Tunis. On Tuesday, 21st of this month, Barbarossa sortied from the town with his Turks to give battle. We attacked and defeated him entirely. A great number of his men fell on the field; we suffered no particular losses. Barbarossa fled, and on that same day we took possession of the town. Because the town's inhabitants did not appear to greet their restored sovereign as they should have done, and as he had a right to expect, we allowed the pillage of the place as punishment for their obstinacy.

Source I: letter from Charles I to his sister Mary, June 1541.

Unless we take immediate action all the estates of Germany may lose their faith, and the Netherlands may follow. After fully considering all these points, I decided to begin by levying war on Hesse and Saxony as disturbers of the peace. . . . This pretext will not long conceal the true purpose of this war of religion, but it will serve to divide the Protestants from the beginning. We shall be able to work out the rest as we go along.

Source J: Charles explains in a letter to Philip (16 February 1546) some of the reasons why he is going to war against the Protestant Schmalkaldic League.

The opportunity which now presents itself should be taken advantage of. We have not only settled the truce with the Turk, but the French have their hands full with the English, besides being in great poverty; and our position towards them is such that it is not probable they would attempt in Germany what at another time they might. We are moreover well armed and prepared for whatever may happen . . . on consideration of all these reasons and others, and in view of His Holiness' offer of aid . . . which will produce a large sum, we conclude that the amount promised by the Pope, with some other funds which we hope to obtain, will be sufficient to cover the estimated cost of maintaining the army for the necessary period.

Questions

1. What was the Schmalkaldic League, referred to in the heading to Source J? (2 marks)
2. How complete a summary of the issues of the imperial election is given by Source F? (4 marks)
3. Judging by its content and tone, how far can Source H be seen as a glorified account of the recapture of Tunis? (4 marks)
*4. Is it possible to discern a difference in tone between the ways in which Charles addresses his brother (Source G) and his sister (Source I)? (5 marks)
5. How far do these sources illustrate the view that Charles' greatest problem was the number of his problems? (10 marks)

Worked answer

*4. [It is reasonable to spend a moment explaining who the two correspondents are, and why there might be a difference in tone, before moving on to look for specific evidence in the extracts. For this many marks, you will have to look closely at what is said, and how.]

Charles' brother Ferdinand was regent for Charles' possessions in Germany, eastern Europe and northern Italy . It has been suggested that it was important to remove Ferdinand from Spain, where he was alarmingly popular, particularly during the troubled first years of Charles' reign. Their sister Mary, following the death in battle of her husband the King of Hungary, became regent in the Netherlands in 1530.

The tone of Source G is tentative: Charles 'advises' and wishes he could 'suggest' ways of dealing with the huge problems of Germany. At the same time, however, he does make clear the key policy elements, and his own commitments as far as the Catholic Church is concerned. In addressing his sister, he merely states the decisions he has reached, although he is aware of the implications for 'her' Netherlands of events in Germany. Charles also takes care to keep his brother up to date with events and developments elsewhere in the empire. He is very frank with his sister about the uncertainties of his position, and the reasons for the deceptions that he is practising.

On the other hand, these are very small examples from a huge and lengthy body of family correspondence, so it is not possible to make definitive statements about the type of letter Charles wrote to each.

6

WHAT PROBLEMS CONFRONTED PHILIP II IN HIS GOVERNMENT OF SPAIN?

BACKGROUND NARRATIVE

Philip ruled Spain from 1543, as regent in the absence of his father and from 1556 he was King. He ruled until his death in 1598 at the age of 71. His last years were spent in almost continuous pain, from arthritis induced by gout. His domestic life was not happy. He outlived his four wives, Mary of Portugal (1543–45), Mary Tudor (1554–58), Elizabeth of Valois (1559–68) and Anne of Austria (1570–80). The only son of his first marriage, usually known as Don Carlos, appears to have been mentally unstable, and died in confinement in 1568, probably of self-inflicted wounds, although trans-European propaganda accused his father of murder. Of his seven other children, only two survived him. Henry Kamen[1] is one of several revisionist historians who describe him as a loving husband, serially distraught by the deaths of his wives. A different view might take into account the brevity of the intervals between his marriages, his frequent absences (on several occasions, on hunting trips) when his children's births were due, and his series of mistresses. Elizabeth of Valois is said to have suffered a miscarriage on seeing the Princess of Ascoli, heavily pregnant, arriving at a royal reception.[2]

The people of Spain were delighted that, unlike his father, Philip spent the whole of his reign, after 1559, in the Iberian peninsula, indeed mostly in Castile. He made three visits to Aragon (1563, 1585–86, 1591) and was in Portugal for two years from 1580, but then returned to Castile, despite having given the Portuguese to understand that he would make Lisbon his capital. Even Castilians saw comparatively little of him, however, since his preferred palaces were away from the big cities, and even when at the Alcázar in Madrid he disliked receiving petitioners, and his methods of work were solitary. At the same time, his court adopted the formal rituals of the Burgundian court.

He followed his father's method of using councils to advise him. The Council of State gave foreign policy advice, but there was also the Council for the Indies, and he established new Councils for Portugal, Italy and Flanders; domestic matters were dealt with by the Councils of Castile and Aragon, and there were separate committees for finance, the Inquisition, the military orders, the law, appointments to offices and so on. Philip did not attend the meetings of these groups, but read the *consultas* which they prepared. This system put considerable power into the hands of the royal secretaries, who assigned the dispatches to the various committees, and took their *consultas* to the King for his comments and final decision. The most notorious example is Antonio Pérez, the illegitimate son of a priest, and of Jewish blood, who nevertheless rose to become one of two royal secretaries, from 1566–79. He was dismissed in 1579, and held in custody. In 1590, Philip's lawyers finally completed an indictment against Pérez, but he escaped from custody in Castile, seeking refuge in his native Aragon.

Despite his distance from his people, Philip suffered only two serious uprisings against him in Spain. Trouble in Granada flared when laws dating back to the 1520s, which prohibited Moorish customs, dress and laws, were finally put into force in 1567. The rebellion that resulted was not completely quelled until November 1570. In Aragon, the presence of the fugitive ex-royal secretary Pérez sparked a rebellion led by unruly nobles, which required military intervention. The loyalty of Aragon's leading aristocratic families helped ensure a rapid royal victory in 1592. As a result, Aragon lost much of its autonomy. One of the reasons for the trouble in Aragon had been the King's use of the Inquisition as a tool of government control. At the same time, Philip regarded the preservation of the Church as one of his most important tasks, and deviancy of all kinds, whether from heretics or from descendants of the Jewish and Muslim populations, was firmly suppressed.

Philip had inherited enormous financial problems, and these worsened throughout his reign; by the time of his last Cortes (1592) he was forced to make constitutional concessions in order to obtain the taxes he needed. Spain itself was experiencing economic problems, exacerbated by the disruption in trade caused by the endless wars, and Philip was forced to declare bankruptcy three times during his reign.

Regardless of its difficulties, Spain retained throughout the reign of Philip a reputation of greatness and glory. The analyses which follow consider the extent to which Philip was motivated by devotion to the Church, and the economic and financial implications of the huge empire overseas over which Castile presided.

ANALYSIS (1): HOW FAR WERE PHILIP'S DOMESTIC POLICIES DOMINATED BY THE CHURCH?

Philip himself would have regarded this question as meaningless. Naturally he was a good son of the Church, and all his actions were informed by an acceptance of the need to do God's work. It is, however, useful to consider the extent to which his policies were aimed directly at the good of the Church, and whether many were not. He was intensely devout. His palace of St Lawrence at El Escorial, on a site chosen in 1561, embodied a monastery and housed his personal collection of 7,000 relics. He had a deep personal commitment to several of the great shrines of Spain, and personally endowed the Shrine of Our Lady of Atocha, a statue said to have been carved by the Evangelist St Luke and miraculously rediscovered after the defeat of the Moors. Other shrines financed by him included those of the Virgin of the Pillar in Saragossa, the Virgin of Montserrat in Catalonia, and Our Lady of Guadalupe in Estremadura. Some of these payments were made at times when the King was desperately short of money for the conduct of national policy. Philip shared with his father a feeling that he had been specifically called to his position by God, and that therefore he could expect divine assistance. 'I don't think that human strength is capable of everything, least of all mine', he said in 1578.[3] Like Charles, Philip was disappointed by his failure to defeat or even contain heresy in his other lands. Just as Charles had reacted to the Reformation in Germany by taking firm action against Protestants in Spain and the Netherlands, so the growing determination of the Netherlands encouraged Philip to be the more orthodox at home.

One field in which his actions coincided with what the Church would have wished was the attack on the increasing *Morisco* population of Spain. The *Moriscos* had, in the 1520s, been allowed a forty-year period of grace, to become accustomed to Christian ways; the expiry of this time limit coincided with the increased determination of the Council of Trent, and with what James Casey calls the 'more combative monarchy' of Philip II.[4] Regulations to prohibit Islamic dress and to force *Moriscos* to adopt a Christian way of life were imposed, and the result was that by the autumn of 1568 open rebellion had broken out in Granada. With the risk that the rebels might obtain help from North Africa and spread their insurrection to the substantial *Morisco* populations of Aragon and Valencia, the government took ruthless action to quell the rebellion. The royal armies occupied the city of Granada, which had been attacked by the rebels in December. The rebel-held mountain stronghold of Alpujarra did not fall until November 1570, by which time thousands had died. Once the last remnants of the rebellion had been crushed, over 80,000 *Moriscos* were expelled from their homes and forcibly resettled in other parts of Spain. It was, wrote the King's half-brother Don Juan, 'the saddest sight in the world, for at the time they set out there was so much rain, wind and snow that mothers had to abandon their children and wives their husbands . . .'.[5] The extent to which this was a 'religious' action has been debated. James Casey has pointed out that the Old Christian landowners of Granada and Valencia were only too happy to use the rebellion and its defeat to extend their own land holdings.[6] The persecution of the *Moriscos* of Spain continued into the next reign, with the expulsion of 275,000 of them to North Africa in 1609–14. The anxiety was always that the conversion of these families was not genuine, and the same worries informed relationships with the *converso* communities. There is no question that many families maintained Judaic practices, informing their children of their Jewish identity only when they were old enough to be discreet. On the other hand, where genuine conversion had occurred – for example, St Teresa of Avila's grandfather had been burned for lapsing into Jewish ways and yet she was undoubtedly Christian – there were still social and career obstacles put in the way of the descendants. Nobility was denied to those whose ancestors had been dealt with by the Inquisition.[7] Philip's handling of his subjects of non-Christian origin was motivated by Christian zeal, rather than regard for the traditions of tolerance which Spain had established since the reign of Ferdinand and Isabella. Economic damage was done to the southern areas of Spain, where the *Morisco* families were the most expert in the necessary techniques of irrigation and fruit tree propagation.

Philip made use of the Holy Office of the Inquisition, not only in his efforts to impose and maintain Catholicism but as a mechanism of social and political control. The general population was prepared to accept the pervasive presence of the Inquisition, in part because the Holy Office targeted others than the loyal and conforming Old Christians. Of those condemned to death between 1570–1610, most were *Moriscos*, foreign immigrants and homosexuals (called 'sodomites') rather than Catholics guilty of blasphemy or superstition. Helen Rawlings suggests even that we can add the entertainment value of the *auto de fé* to this equation, which helped to ensure that the Inquisition became 'a respected agent of royal authority'.[8] The Inquisition was used in this way, for example, in dealing with the rebellion in Aragon, which was sparked by the escape from custody of Antonio Pérez, and by the Inquisition's attempt to recapture him. Once the royal armies had succeeded in bringing Aragon back under control, the Inquisition reminded the population that obedience to the King was their Christian duty. The influence of the Inquisition was also positive, particularly in the field of religious education: the Toledo Inquisitorial Tribunal at the end of Philip's reign found that, by 1599, 82 per cent of those interrogated could say their prayers accurately, compared to 75 per cent in 1575 and fewer than 40 per cent before 1555.[9]

Thus Philip acted as a good son of the Church. This did not, however, guarantee the approval of the Papacy for all of his actions. Indeed, until Philip cast himself in the role of the sword of Rome against England, there were long periods of hostility between the Vatican and Spain. And there were many other issues dominating Philip's government as it attempted to rule Spain, in dealing with which even the Inquisition was not enough. Philip had read and studied a great deal about the Revolt of the *Comuñeros*, and throughout his reign he was determined to avoid the kind of widespread rebellion which had threatened his father's early years. To do this, he needed to maintain the loyalty of the dominant groups in Spanish society. After all, Kings of Spain were not anointed; their royal authority came from the oaths they swore to their Cortes, and political philosophers in sixteenth-century Spain, such as Vives, even defended the theory of tyrannicide. One way in which Philip could hope to maintain control of his kingdoms was to keep the nobles loyal. Ferdinand and Isabella had worked hard to reduce the power of the nobility, using *letrados* in all the departments of government. But as the sale of offices became necessary because of Philip's financial problems, the *hidalgo* class began to gain power. And even where his civil servants were not noble, Philip's companions were. The most significant personality of the first half of the reign was the Prince of Eboli, Ruy Gómez de Silva. Gómez, until his death in 1573, was Chief Gentleman of the Bedchamber, and so in charge of all Philip's most intimate and domestic moments. All the nobles liked to be at court, because that was where they could have access to favours, pensions and sinecures. Like Louis XIV at Versailles later, the King could punish bad behaviour by exiling people from the court. The King's court became 'a magnet for the ambitious, a place where they would go to celebrate the great feasts and to manoeuvre for honours and posts of command. Philip was inundated with petitions for favours',[10] and one of the aims of his government was to keep the nobility occupied in such harmless rivalry. It was harmless, because Philip ensured that the nobles continued to be subject to the law. One reason for the handsome buildings for the Law Courts in Granada was to demonstrate how important the law was, and that it was superior to all. The rebellion in Aragon, and the difficulty with which it was quelled, confirmed that the greatest danger to the King could arise when one of his close associates turned against him.

Philip's main preoccupation, however, for much of his reign, was the collection of revenue. His expenditure seldom bore any logical relationship to his resources, and shortage of money was a perennial problem. Revenues from various Church sources were much less valuable than they had been during the reigns of his father and great-grandparents, amounting to less that 1.6 million ducats out of a total of almost 10 million ducats. The hostility of the Council of Trent to the issue of blanket indulgences like the *cruzada* had reduced its value, and the *subsidio*, the royal share of tithe, brought in less than 400,000 ducats a year. The Papacy also authorised the collection of the *excusado*, but this brought in even less.[11] Indeed, the collection of revenue was a secular preoccupation, with issues of morality normally disregarded by the Council of Finance, which Philip had inherited from his father, as it grappled with crisis after crisis. Four times during his reign Philip was compelled to suspend or reschedule his debt payments. The bankruptcies (1557, 1560, 1575 and 1596) were proof of his difficulties, yet he was never able to adjust his expenditure to his probable income. One of his many nicknames may have been that of 'the prudent King', but his policies and personal extravagances together put an insupportable burden on the taxpayers of Castile. The most significant of the indirect taxes, the *alcabalá*, was raised on several occasions, but the decision in 1575 to collect it at the maximum rate of 10 per cent met with such opposition that, in 1577, the representatives of the cities agreed to vote more *servicios* in return for the right to administer the taxation system themselves. Tax revenue in 1577 had increased by 50 per cent over 1567 levels.[12] Even this was not enough, and in 1589 the Cortes agreed to a new tax, the *millones*, despite the awareness that a tax on the most basic necessities of life was unjust. This levy on purchases of items like wine, oil, meat and vinegar was made the more unfair by the fact that it was levied according to census figures of the 1530s, which were thus 50 years out of date.

It would be anachronistic to expect a 'Christian prince' of the sixteenth century to regard the care of his fellow men as a key Christian obligation. In his personal life, and by his own values, Philip attempted with every action to fulfil his duties to God. But, as with all his policies, crisis management and a desperate search for income prevented any serious focus on the real secular and religious needs of his people.

ANALYSIS (2): DID SPAIN'S OVERSEAS POSSESSIONS STRENGTHEN OR WEAKEN SPAIN DURING THE REIGN OF PHILIP II?

For contemporaries, there was no question that the overseas possessions of Spain were its greatest strength. After the Portuguese accession in 1580, the Spanish empire extended across the whole world, and encompassed the sources of all the riches then known to man: gold and silver from the Andes, pearls from the Pacific coast of America, jewels, spices and fine textiles from Asia. Across Europe, the Spanish ruled the wealthy commercial Netherlands, and the key cities in the north and south of Italy (Milan and Naples). And Castilians had the best of both worlds: their King was the most powerful on earth and yet, unlike his father, he stayed where he belonged, among them, rather than visiting his overseas possessions. Indeed, except for his time in Portugal (1581–83), Philip did not leave Spain once he had returned from his visit to Germany and the Netherlands in 1559.

The wishes expressed by Spaniards ever since the Revolt of the *Comuñeros* were fulfilled. The King realised that the government could not be perpetually on the move. His predecessors had begun the process of settling the administration: since the fifteenth century the *Chancillería*, or High Court, had been permanently in Valladolid, although a branch of the court was set up in Granada to ensure access for the citizens of southern Spain; the State Archive had, since 1547, been in Simancas. In 1561, Philip completed the process, by the decision to make a permanent capital in Madrid: while it was a smaller town than some, the air was good, high in the hills; there was better water than in Toledo and

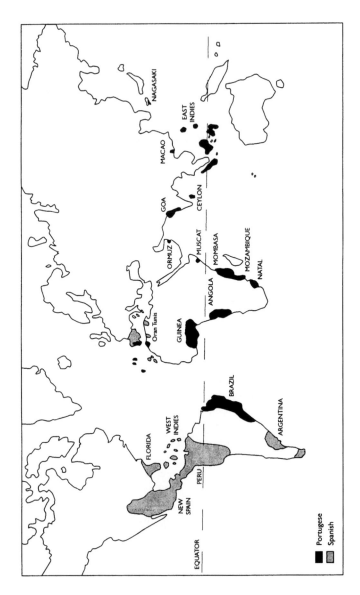

Map 6.1 The Empire of Spain after 1580

more timber for building than in Valladolid. From his homes, first in the Alcazar in Madrid, and then at the Escorial, about 40 kilometres from Madrid, he ruled his wide empire while remaining at home.

The overseas possessions of Spain strengthened, above all, Spain's status as the greatest power in Europe. The settlements in America extended from modern-day California in the north, to the areas of Argentina which lay to the south of the Tropic of Capricorn. It seemed to the other maritime nations of Europe that soon all the world would be controlled by Spain. And these holdings were not just sterile marks on the new maps. They provided a new home for some of Spain's citizens as well as a substantial market for European commodities. Above all, the great wealth of all the world poured into Spain. But these strengths were also damaging to Spain. As we shall see in Chapter 7, the animosity of the rest of Europe was one of the reasons for the very expensive foreign wars which occupied almost every year of Philip's reign.

The issue of emigration was a complex one. The Spanish government tried to ensure that all those who emigrated were of sound moral and religious character, and the *Casa de Contratacion* in Seville issued licences for emigration only to citizens of Castilian Christian blood. This is in marked contrast to the colonial policies of other nations, both then and since: the Kings of France allowed some of their Huguenot subjects to attempt to set up a colony in South America, and the first successful English colonists in North America were refugee puritans. In the eighteenth and nineteenth centuries, both England and France were to use their overseas possessions as convict settlements. The effect of Spain's careful policy was to damage the normal demographic development of the country, and may be one of the reasons that Spain's population ceased to grow by the end of the century. James Casey[13] suggests that, in the second half of the sixteenth century, between 4,000 and 5,000 people left every year to settle in America. At this time, there were probably 200,000 young men in Spain, and the emigration of so many of them – for the typical emigrant was a single man in his late teens or early twenties – had an adverse effect on population growth. Despite all that the Council of the Indies could do, there were rich opportunities to be exploited in the empire, and land with the natives to work it continued to be available. Although missionaries also went to America, and attempted to improve the lot of the native people, the crown needed the revenue from the settlers and their bonded *encomendero* serfs.

The wealth of America fell into the hands of Spain with the easy conquest of Mexico by Hernán Cortés and his band of fewer than 1,000 men, and the even more startling taking of Peru by Pizarro and his handful of followers. Charles I had tried to establish the systems which would contain these unruly conquistadors, and set up an empire of justice and fraternity: the New Laws of 1542, and the unremitting attempts of the Council of the Indies struggled to maintain the rule of law. But in the end, the key function of empire was to supply wealth. The first enormous windfall had been the ransom paid by the Inca warlord Atahuallpa, valued at something approaching $1,000 million at modern gold prices. After that, the amount of bullion reaching Spain rose throughout the century. At Philip's accession, the annual amount was about 10.5 million pesos. By the 1570s, the amount had risen to almost 30 million pesos, and in the 1590s it reached almost 70 million pesos. The crown's share was always around 30 per cent of the total.[14] The rest of Europe assumed Spain to be a nation of wealthy men, and the King of Spain to be the richest of all. Indeed, American silver amounted to about one-fifth of all the annual royal revenues in the last two decades of Philip's reign. (As a comparison, we may note that, at the height of the North Sea oil 'boom' of the 1980s, which fuelled the low taxation policies of the British government under Margaret Thatcher, income from all gas and oil sources was approximately15 per cent[15]).

Despite the envy of the rest of Europe, much of this money did not reach Spain. Philip was forced to follow his father's borrowing policies; indeed, the effective loss of the northern Netherlands, and royal reluctance to antagonise the southern provinces meant that Spain was the only source of tax revenue; the costs of war could be met only by borrowing. Annuities raised some money from the wealthy in Spain, but most of the money came from the German bankers, whose interest was paid, under the *asiento* arrangement, by the direct forwarding of whole shiploads of treasure. The precarious nature of the royal finances could be seen whenever anything went wrong with the flow of specie (coin), whether through piracy, adverse weather or merely late sailing from the Caribbean. The silver which was unloaded in Spain had the effect of feeding the inflation which had beset the country during the reign of Charles I. The availability of coins was bound to drive rising prices ever higher, particularly given the shortage of commodities. And the overseas empire was one reason for this shortage. The demand for textiles in the New World continued to be insatiable, increasingly met by imported cloth from the Netherlands and even England. In addition, as young men left the land, whether to emigrate, or merely to seek their fortunes in the trading cities of Cadiz and Seville, shortage of agricultural products worsened. In years of drought or plague, the towns could not be fed without the expedient of importing Calabrian grain, and thus prices continued to rise.

Paradoxically, then, the great empire may have damaged mainland Spain more than it strengthened her. By enhancing the envy of other nations, and the number of fronts on which Spain was vulnerable to attack, it increased the already enormous overspending on foreign policy which so unbalanced the revenues of the kingdom. At the same time, the effect on Spanish currency lessened the purchasing power of the crown's revenues, and increased the difficulties of supplying the cities and armies of Spain. Although Spain was to maintain its hold on its overseas empire until the early years of the nineteenth century, these lands rapidly became more of a burden than a benefit.

Questions

1. How and for what reasons did Spain become and remain an imperial power during the sixteenth century?
2. In what ways and to what extent were the lives of the native people affected by Spanish expansion in the New World to 1660? (AEB Summer 1997)

SOURCES

1. PHILIP'S METHODS OF GOVERNMENT

Source A: the Venetian Ambassador Suriano reports to the Senate of Venice, 1559.

Although his time of life is apt to engender an insatiable desire to govern, his efforts are directed not to increase his possessions by war but to preserve them by peace ... although he resembles his father in his features, he is dissimilar in many respects ... the Emperor governed entirely according to his own views, but the King governs according to the views of others, and he has no esteem for any nation except the Spanish. He consorts only with Spaniards, and with these only he takes counsel and governs.

Source B: Gonzalo Perez considers the methods of the King in 1565.

In many things His Majesty makes and will make mistakes, because he discusses matters with several people, now with one, then with another, hiding something from one but revealing it to others, and so it is no surprise that differing and even contradictory letters emerge, and this happens not just in Flanders but in other provinces as well. This cannot fail to cause great harm and many problems.

Source C: speech by the King's Minister, Eraso, at the opening of the Cortes of Castile (Córdoba 1570).

The King as you know has resided throughout these years in Spain, although there were grave and pressing reasons for his leaving in order to attend in person to matters in others of his states, as was made clear ... in the last Cortes. But His Majesty knows how necessary his presence is in these kingdoms ... not only for their own good and advantage, but also to provide ... for the needs of the other States, for these kingdoms, of all his dominions, are the vital centre, the head and principal part. And considering also the great love he bears you, His Majesty so ordered matters that while remedies to instant necessity were to be sought, his absence from Spain might be avoided.

Source D: the Cortes of Valencia in 1585.

We can boast that we have never witnessed nor lived under a king and lord who so earnestly and with such care and solicitude, looks to the welfare and proper government of his subjects and vassals.

Questions

1. Explain what the Ambassador means by 'his time of life' (Source A) (2 marks)
2. To what extent do Sources A and B agree about how Philip I governed? (4 marks)
3. For what reasons and to what extent is Source D unlikely to be reliable as an expression of the views of all Philip's Iberian subjects? (5 marks)
4. Discuss and account for the difference in tone between Sources B and C. (6 marks)
5*. By using your own knowledge, discuss the extent to which these sources confirm that Philip's methods of government were different from those of his predecessors. (8 marks)

Worked answer

*5. *[The instruction to 'use your own knowledge' does not alter the need to study and refer in detail to each of the sources in turn; it is also essential to reach a firm conclusion after you have considered all the sources, rather than merely letting your answer end once you have commented on Source D.]*

Source A's suggestion that Philip did not want to extend his territories by war certainly differentiates him from his predecessors: both Ferdinand

and Charles regarded war as an extension of policy, and extended their territory, mostly at the expense of France. On the other hand, Philip's lack of expansionist ambition did not mean that he was able to keep his lands at peace. Source A also describes Charles as making entirely his own decisions, which is clearly not true, since he delegated to regents as he moved around his territories. First his wife, Isabella, and then his son had been left in charge of Spain, with little more than general advice to guide them. Ferdinand and Isabella's circumstances were different, but they certainly did collude over the government and decision making in their kingdoms. Similarly, they took advice, notably from churchmen such as Cisneros.

Philip's preference for Spaniards and his 'great love' for them, as mentioned in Source C, is well attested, and in this he did differ from his father; Charles' preference for Flemish advisers, at least in the first part of his reign, is well known, and he continued to choose advisers from all his territories. His linguistic skills made this possible for him, as it was not for his son. Philip's willingness to listen to, or more probably read, advice is confirmed in Source B, and it is not something that Charles had time for. Source B also reminds us that Philip had other provinces to deal with as did Charles; but he never took as personal an interest in his foreign holdings as Charles did. Above all, as Source C makes clear, Philip stayed in Iberia for almost all of his reign, after his five years in the Netherlands; indeed, except for a few brief visits to the kingdom of Aragon, and a short stay in Portugal, he remained in Castile for almost all of his reign.

Source D suggests that the use of the Cortes was a commonplace; but Philip, like his predecessors, used the Castilian Cortes much more frequently than he used those of the kingdom of Aragon. Indeed he, like Charles and Ferdinand and Isabella, preferred to limit the authority of the Cortes, by controlling the membership, and minimising the number of times they were called. The loyal words of the Cortes of Valencia contrasted with its reluctance to provide the funds for which it was asked, and the same was true during earlier reigns. Charles managed to avoid asking the Spanish Cortes to impose new taxes, as he was able to collect revenue in the Netherlands; Philip found increasingly that all his revenues had to come from Castile, as this was the most biddable of his territories.

Philip's methods were different from those of Ferdinand who, after all, ruled Castile on sufferance, and Charles, who saw Spain as merely one of many provinces. Philip's full attention was focused on Spain and its needs: as Source B implies, there were times when a little less concentration might have been welcome to the Spanish administrators.

2. SOME OF THE PROBLEMS CONFRONTING PHILIP

Source E: petition from Francisco Nunez Mulay, *Morisco* noble, to the President of the High Court of Justice against the new laws proclaimed in Granada January 1567.

When the naturals of this kingdom were converted to the Christian faith, there was no regulation compelling them to abandon their dress, language or customs associated with their festivities; and indeed that conversion was forced and against the agreed surrender terms. . . . What good would come from forcing us to keep the doors of our houses open? It would allow thieves to rob us and the lustful to have access to women. . . . If anyone wanted to be a Moor and follow their ceremonies, couldn't they do so at night? Of course they could! Islam requires solitude and retreat. Therefore it matters little whether doors are opened or closed if the intention is there; there is punishment for him who does what he should not, for nothing is concealed from God. . . . To require our women to unveil their faces is only to provide opportunity for men to sin after beholding the beauty of those they are attracted to; while the ugly will find no-one willing to marry them. They cover themselves because they do not want to be known, just like Christian women; it is an act of modesty to avoid molestation. . . . Our ancient surnames serve to identify people and preserve lineage. What could be gained by losing these records? . . . But the greatest inconvenience of all would be the loss of our Arabic language. How can a language be taken away from a people, the natural language in which they are reared? . . . This is clearly a measure designed to weaken us . . . and those who could not sustain such hardship would leave the land or become brigands . . .

Source F: Dutch propaganda about Philip II's treatment of his oldest son.

John, the third of that name, succeeded . . . in the Kingdom . . . who by Katherine his wife had many children which died all in their infancies, except Prince John and Mary. The which Mary married Philip, now King and then Prince of Castile, and died before her said husband came to his crown, leaving only one son, whose name was Charles. Whom, as the fame thereof is constant, his father King Philip commanded to be put to death in prison.

Source G: Philip's personal memorandum on whether to increase the *alcabalá* or put a tax on flour, 1574.

And it is quite clear that there is more reason for choosing the *alcabalás* rather than the flour. Flour has to be paid for by both rich and poor, since the poor man has to eat just like the rich man. This doesn't happen with the *alcabalá*, which is paid according to the quantity of goods that is bought or sold, which means that the rich man pays more and the poor man less.... The matter has many obstacles to get thorough, and even if it gets through the committees, there are still the Cortes deputies and then the cities, which is worse.

Source H: dealing with the riots in Aragon, 1591: Philip's letter to the *junta* on Aragon.

I don't believe there is anyone in the world so blind or so misinformed as not to understand perfectly well the responsibility thrust on me in Aragon; and much less those here in the *junta*.... I understand perfectly well this responsibility I now have, and the greatest responsibility of all is the service of Our Lord.... There is the responsibility that I also have to the administration of justice in that kingdom and the punishment of those who have put both Inquisition and justice in the condition in which they are.... I am determined to resolve this as necessary, even if it means involving my own person and whatever else is required. If for the sake of religion we have been through and done what you have seen in Flanders and then in France, the responsibility is even greater to our own people on our own doorstep. For I see very well that if you abandon them and do not help them as you should, they will attempt to abolish the Inquisition.... For all these reasons I cannot but be very firm and determined in what I have said. It also seems desirable that before any resort to force other appropriate means be explored, in order to achieve peacefully what I have been saying. But these means must be through the due and fitting use of authority, not through the pardon that I think some of you have proposed ...

Source H: the Duke of Gandia, in a letter to a friend, 1591, comments on the troubles in Aragon.

If this matter of Aragon should reach breaking point I would not count much on those in Castile, for not only are those who have complaints about the burdens and taxes of these last few years happy to spread it around by word of mouth, they even publish it with posters that they have put up in Seville and Avila; and you know the disturbance they caused in Madrid. I also beg you consider what assurance there is that the Portuguese stay quiet, and how things are going in Italy. The affairs of Flanders, France and Italy speak for themselves on the little need the King has to seek another war.

Questions

*1. Identify John III, Prince John and Mary (Source F) (3 marks)
2. How far was Philip's opinion of the *alcabalá* (Source G) shared by the people of Castile? (3 marks)

3. Discuss the significance of the Inquisition and of the *junta* in both bringing about and then dealing with the riots in Aragon. (4 marks)
4. Explain and comment on the points made by Mulay (Source E). To what extent does this letter suggest that the new legislation was both unjust and unnecessary? (7 marks)
5. How far do these sources confirm or refute the suggestion that only in the last decade of Philip's reign did problems begin to surface? (8 marks)

Worked answer

1*. *[Remember that brief but clear explanations are all that are required in these introductory questions; the purpose of this question is to ensure that you can disentangle Philip's marriages, and that you will not confuse his two wives called Mary.]*

John III was the King of Portugal from 1521 to 1557; his sister was Philip II's mother.

Prince John, his son, died in 1554, leaving a posthumous child, Sebastian, who came to the throne on his grandfather's death.

John III's daughter Mary married her first cousin Philip in 1543, dying in childbirth two years later at the age of 17.

7

THE SUCCESSES AND FAILURES OF PHILIP II's FOREIGN POLICY

BACKGROUND NARRATIVE

Philip ruled not only Spain, but also the Netherlands, the duchy of Burgundy, the Italian states of Milan, Naples and Sicily, and the empire in America. He had hoped to take over all his father's lands, but in the event the Habsburg hereditary lands, together with the Holy Roman Empire, went to his uncle Ferdinand. Foreign policy was not his forté. As Fernand Braudel points out: 'Despite his quite extensive travels – through Germany and Flanders, with visits to Italy and England, between 1548 and 1559 – he never managed to speak a modern foreign language.'[1] Even in Portugal, the land of his mother and his nurse, he could understand but not speak the language. With his inheritance came the long-standing conflict with France, but this was to be the least of his foreign policy problems: the death of Henry II in 1559 brought to France half-a-century of weak or underage monarchs, and of religious strife. While Philip became involved, sending assistance to the Guise-led Catholic League, he faced much greater, and more expensive, problems elsewhere.

War in the Mediterranean occupied Philip's resources for the first half of his reign. As well as attacking Muslim strongholds in North Africa, Philip's fleet was victorious over the Ottoman fleet at Lepanto in 1571. Following the battle, the Turks concentrated their attention in the Balkans, and thus became the problem of Philip's Habsburg cousins. Trouble in the Netherlands proved to be much more intractable and therefore costly, in terms both of finance and of prestige. Organised rebellion began in 1567, and the rebels were strengthened by the Union of Utrecht of 1579, a Protestant reaction to the Catholic Union of Arras. In 1581, the Estates of the United Provinces deposed Philip II, and until the end of his life, Philip fought without success to restore his hold on his father's homeland. The Dutch were helped by the English Queen Elizabeth, and one of the most remarkable aspects of Philip's foreign affairs is the diplomatic revolution which turned England from allies into implacable enemies. Uneasy relationships during the 1550s and 1560s were worsened by Elizabeth's marital advances towards Protestant and even French princes, but the war was triggered by a combination of commercial disputes, the situation of the heir-apparent Mary, Queen of Scots, and Elizabeth's assistance to the Dutch. Open war broke out in 1585, and continued to the end of the reigns of both Philip and Elizabeth, despite the defeat of Spain's great Armada in 1588. Professor Geoffrey Parker argues convincingly that Philip's policies can be explained by what he calls 'prospect theory'. He says that 'not wanting to lose' is a much stronger motivation than 'wanting to win' and that individuals 'are disposed to pay a higher price and run higher risks when they face losses than when they seek gains . . . conflicts tend to be more common – and to last longer – when both sides believe that they are defending the status quo, because each believes it will suffer losses until it takes strong if not aggressive action'.[2] Certainly, the eventual twelve-year truce of 1609 embodied the demands which the Dutch rebels had made more than twenty years earlier, and continuing war against England impoverished Spain as much as it did England.

Protestant propaganda ensured, for many years, that Philip was anathematised. His three main antagonists, Henry of Navarre, Elizabeth I of England and William of Orange, became, as Henry Kamen points out, 'legendary heroes in the memory of their own people'.[3] As late as 1856, the historian J. L. Motley memorably demonised him: 'If there are vices . . . from which he was exempt, it is because it is not permitted by human nature to attain perfection even in evil'.[4] His lack of success whenever he confronted Protestant enemies, with their powerful propaganda machines, is one reason for such hostility. The two analyses which follow consider why the long drawn out war in the Netherlands resulted in failure for Spain, and the extent to which religion was a key element in Philip's conduct of foreign policy.

ANALYSIS (1): WHY WAS PHILIP II UNABLE TO RETAIN CONTROL OF HIS LANDS IN THE NETHERLANDS?

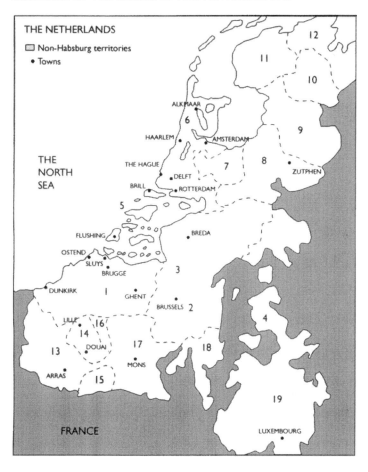

Provinces

1 Flanders (Dutch Speaking)	8 Guelderland	15 Cambrai
2 Brabant	9 Overyssel	16 Tournai
3 Mechlin	10 Drente	17 Hainault
4 Limburg	11 Friesland	18 Namur
5 Zealand	12 Gröningen	19 Luxembourg
6 Holland	13 Artois	
7 Utrecht	14 Flanders (French Speaking)	

Map 7.1 The Netherlands

The Netherlands were the only part of his far-flung territories that Philip II effectively lost during his reign, and yet at the time of his accession many would have said that these were among the most secure of his holdings. Charles I had regarded the Netherlands as his homeland, and it was the only province outside Spain in which Philip spent a significant amount of time: he was based in Flanders between 1555 and 1559, and frequently promised the States General that he would return, although he never did. Indeed, after September 1559, he never left the Iberian peninsula again. Perhaps more remarkably, he remained in central Castile, where messengers had the maximum distance to cover by slow land transport, rather than settling, for example, near the Atlantic or the Mediterranean coast, to facilitate communications.

Philip's view was straightforward: the Netherlands came to him in direct line from his father and grandfather. They were to be ruled, as they had been since 1506, by governors appointed by the King. And, as Philip wrote to the King of Denmark in 1586, referring to the widely accepted Confession of Augsburg (1555): 'if it is clear that other sovereigns do not allow their subjects to have a religion other than the one they themselves profess, for reasons of state as well as for religious motives, why should this attitude be denied to me?'.[5] Despite his confidence, by 1566 the Netherlands were in open revolt against his government, and Philip never recovered full control. These demands began with the issue of religious tolerance, but rapidly extended to an insistence on autonomy, and in 1581 Philip was formally deposed as ruler by the rebels. Although the independence of the northern Netherlands was not to be fully recognised until the middle of the seventeenth century, they had in fact ceased to be part of the Spanish empire.

The absence of their ruler may have been one cause of the escalating troubles in the Netherlands. This had not been a problem in the reign of Charles, in part because of the personal affection felt for him, and his willingness to respond to complaints, for example over the issue of taxation. But the main reason was that the governors appointed by Charles were able to rule unimpeded in his absence. Philip, as Geoffrey Parker has shown so lucidly, could not resist the urge to 'micromanage',[6] while at the same time he failed to define the parameters within which his orders could be adjusted without consultation. This kind of government was impossible given the fact that 'Spain waged an unremitting struggle against the obstacles of distance'.[7] For instance, when in 1573 Philip wrote a letter telling the Duke of Alba to 'gain days, hours and even moments in what must be done', the courier took six weeks to reach Alba in Brussels.[8] Systems of government had been elaborated during Charles' reign. A *Reichkreis*, or central committee, of the seventeen provinces had been formed in 1548, but each province remained very self aware, and the States General's legislation was not binding unless it was accepted by the Assembly of each. The Council of State, made up of nobles, meanwhile resented the lawyers and clerics who formed the royal civil service.

Religion was, however, the main pretext for anti-Spanish feeling. Charles had allowed established inquisitors at the diocesan level to deal with Lutheran heresy as early as 1522, but the followers of John Calvin proved much more intractable. The nobility of the Netherlands were, in the main, Catholic, but their education was Erasmian, and they were inclined to tolerance. They were also infuriated at the papal announcement of 1561. Aware that the Netherlands did not have enough bishops for efficient pastoral care, Philip had agreed the establishment of fourteen new dioceses, one of them an archdiocese. The fact that these appointments were made and announced without consulting or even informing the Council of State in the Netherlands was, at the least, tactless. Greater Catholic presence was needed, but these appointments came too late, and Calvinism had taken a strong hold in many of the cities of the Netherlands. In 1566 came the Iconoclastic Fury, when mobs attacked the churches and destroyed many of the images or, as they declared, idols, with which they were adorned. Such mob violence should have been quickly and cleanly put down, but the Spanish government did not have sufficient troops in the Netherlands. The reign had begun with a small standing army, but this had been disbanded for reasons of economy, and thus troops had to be brought from Italy or Spain.

Attempts to tax the Netherlands in order to cover their own defence, as well as their own policing, were also unpopular. Alba's attempt, in 1571, to introduce a new tax known as the Tenth Penny, was so unpopular that it was abandoned the next year. The rebels pointed out that it was a version of the Castilian *alcabalá* – a powerful propaganda point. The new tax was one of the reasons why the *Gueux*, a group of Calvinist seamen, were able to seize and hold the port of Brill, from where they preyed on Spanish shipping. The second bankruptcy of the crown, in 1575, also had disastrous consequences in the Netherlands, since unpaid Spanish troops sacked Antwerp (the so-called Spanish Fury) ruining the prosperous town and alienating both Catholics and Protestants. Ortiz de Zúñiga, writing in 1677, described the struggle in the Netherlands as 'the graveyard of our armies, the swallowing up of our treasure, the interruption of our progress and well being'.[9]

The leadership of the local nobility was also decisive in stirring revolution. Although many of them were Catholic, they resented foreign taxation and foreign rule, and their attitude angered both Philip and Alba.

In 1568, two leading nobles, the Counts of Egmont and Hoorn, were executed by order of the so-called Council of Blood, and immediately became martyrs to the cause. Their place at the head of the burgeoning rebellion was taken by William of Nassau, Prince of Orange, who was to become the first Stadtholder of the United Provinces when they declared their independence at the Union of Utrecht in 1579. As early as 1567, it was suggested to Philip that the assassination of the Prince of Orange would be wise; while Philip rejected the idea then, further attempts were made and the successful assassin of Orange in 1584 was rewarded by the Spanish government.[10]

If the leadership of the rebels was divided, the leadership of the Spanish response was far from united and consistent. Philip at times wondered whether moderation would be better than stringency. By replacing his aunt Margaret of Parma with the Duke of Alba, he ensured a militaristic response to problems. Later, his appointment of the more moderate Duke of Medinaceli, to replace the Duke of Alba, was done in secret, with different instructions being sent by courier to Alba from those which Medinaceli himself received. And whoever was ruling the Netherlands, the advice, instructions and changes of policy came from Madrid with every courier. What did not come, however, was sufficient funds to deal with the rebellion. By December 1572, Alba owed his Spanish troops twenty months' wages, and it is estimated that the monthly cost of the fighting in the Netherlands in 1572–73 was 500,000 ducats.[11] Since the total revenue of the King amounted to 6 million ducats, of which half went on interest payments, it is clear that the cost of the war was crippling.

One reason for these costs was beyond the control of either side. The developments in military theory of the 1520s had resulted in radical changes in the fortifications which had been implemented by Charles, and indeed by Philip, to protect the cities of the Netherlands from attack by the French. The star-shaped fortifications, with their ravelins and overlapping fields of fire made cities almost impregnable, and thus sieges lasted much longer and were more expensive. Antwerp, for example, held out for a year against the might of Spain in 1584–85. When such cities did fall, the brutality ordered by Alba may have made some towns surrender, but it is also clear that others held out even longer, realising that they had nothing to lose. In contrast, we may note that Philip was not prepared to carry brutality to extremes. The suggestion that he should order the flooding of the entire coastal plain might have resulted in the ruin and capitulation of the rebels. But Philip refused to countenance the idea. Of course, since he was confident that he would regain full control, it was not in his interests to destroy the fragile ecology of these lands.

Philip was also unable to provide a North Sea fleet to counteract the *Gueux* and their allies, the English, although from the mid-1580s, the Duke of Parma did begin to build up shipping.[12] Philip's main navy was based in the Mediterranean, and he could not move it from there. When the Netherlands began to force themselves onto his agenda in the mid-1560s, Philip was already engaged in extensive, and ongoing, commitments against the Turks and their allies in the Mediterranean. Even after Malta was relieved in 1565, the Granada revolt (1568–70) and the Lepanto campaign (1571) tied up Spain's resources, precluding any major switch of attention to the north. He was at the same time helping the King of France, his brother-in-law, against the Protestants. Possibly a more single-minded approach to the trouble in the Netherlands at that early stage might have saved them for him permanently. If Philip was giving assistance to the King of France, the Netherlands in their turn were getting assistance from other Protestant countries. Without the help, at first tacit and then open, of Elizabeth of England, the Netherlands would have been less able to resist and so to achieve victory. Elizabeth allowed refugees to settle, and to recruit in England. Her harbours became bases for Dutch privateers, and her own favourite, the Earl of Leicester, led troops against the Spanish in the Netherlands. When the hostility between England and Spain turned to open warfare, it could only help the cause of Dutch independence.

However much leadership, motivation and religious zeal the Netherlanders had, no-one really believed that they could resist the most powerful monarch in Europe, nor withstand the largest army and navy in the known world. And yet, when, in 1590, Philip resignedly told the Pope that he intended to extend tolerance to the Dutch, it was too late to regain full control over the northern Netherlands. The lands which became known as the Austrian Netherlands consisted of less than half the 'Burgundian lands' which Philip had inherited from his father. The determination of the Dutch, and their powerful foreign supporters, coupled with the fatal inability of Philip to delegate or to compromise, resulted in the loss of the richest part of the European empire of Spain.

Questions

1. Why did rebellion break out in the Netherlands by 1566? (OCR Summer 1998)
2. Why, despite the enormous odds against them, did the Dutch rebels secure, by 1609, substantial victory over Spain? (AEB Summer 1998)

ANALYSIS (2): TO WHAT EXTENT WAS RELIGION A MOTIVE FORCE IN PHILIP II'S FOREIGN POLICY?

As we noted in Chapter 6, this question would have appeared meaningless to Philip II himself, who regarded himself as the sword of God throughout his reign. His propagandists referred to him as King David, and the motto *Non sufficit orbis* ('The earth is not enough') was engraved on various pamphlets and placards. Philip's commitment to holding on to all his territories was derived partly from his conviction that he had been chosen by God to rule them. He always, however, had other motives for what he did, and there were occasions when his religious policies were compromised by other imperatives. In the American empire, for example, the missionaries were very much against the bondage system of the *repartimiento*, by which native Americans were allocated to labour for Spanish settlers. Philip nevertheless continued to authorise serfdom rather than risk rebellion from the *creoles*, the families of Spanish blood.

The constant war against the Ottoman Turks can be seen as a religious crusade. On the other hand, the security of the Mediterranean continued to be crucial to Philip, as it had been to his predecessors. Throughout his reign, therefore, Philip sought to preserve the shipping lanes between Spain and Naples, and to protect the grain and other ships of the western Mediterranean against the North African pirates and their Turkish overlord. Although the great naval victory at Lepanto in 1571 reduced the danger of a Turkish attack, it did not eliminate it, and Philip was compelled always to have troops and ships available in the Mediterranean.

In the rest of Europe, too, the requirements of religion often overlapped with the needs of other policy, and were on occasion completely irrelevant to Philip's endeavours. The taking of Portugal was a matter of dynastic ambition rather than of religion. When Philip's nephew Sebastian died in battle in North Africa in 1578, the throne of Portugal was disputed. Sebastian's uncle Henry, a Cardinal, claimed the throne and immediately tried to persuade the Pope to release him from his vows so that he could produce an heir. But he was already an old man, and was challenged by Anthony, Prior of Crato, the son of Henry's elder brother Luis. The problem was that Anthony was illegitimate, and the resulting uncertainty provided Philip with the opportunity to claim Portugal for his own. In 1580, with the death of Henry, Philip seized the throne. The Portuguese Cortes argued in vain that the female line (through which Philip claimed) was invalid in Portugal. Many powerful nobles, such as the Duke of Albuquerque, supported the Spanish claim, and Anthony, who had rashly sought refuge in Castile with his 'proofs of legitimacy' when his Uncle

Henry had rejected his claim, had no choice but to escape. The defeat, in 1582, of Prince Anthony's fleet at the Azores, despite the fact that some English ships were in support, followed by the recapture of the island of Terceira in 1583, established Philip securely on the throne of Portugal.

Religion was, however, the key issue in the Netherlands, as we have seen. The antipathy between the Netherlanders and their distant ruler was sparked and fed by religious differences, and Philip felt inadequately supported by the Pope as he struggled to save the souls of his Dutch subjects. The Pope was much more enthusiastic when it came to what Philip called the 'Enterprise of England', which adopted many of the characteristics of a crusade. In 1567, Philip went against established diplomatic protocol when he ordered the English Ambassador in Madrid, Dr Man, to cease his private Protestant worship and to accept Catholic Mass. The expulsion of Dr Man from Madrid is seen by some as the first stage in the English–Spanish hostility which was to last throughout the rest of the reign. The Pope had wanted to excommunicate Elizabeth I in 1563, at which point Philip had dissuaded him, arguing that Elizabeth, a woman and therefore weak, would eventually be persuaded to resume the practice of the true religion. He did not approve of the Bull *Regnans in Excelsis*, which eventually excommunicated Elizabeth in 1571, but by then it had become clear than only force of arms would rescue England from heresy. In that year Philip wrote: 'I am so keen to achieve the consummation of this enterprise, I am so attached to it in my heart, and I am so convinced that God our Saviour must embrace it as His own cause, that I cannot be dissuaded.'[13] The Armada, when it finally sailed in 1588, had more priests than doctors, its banners blessed by the Pope and the confidence of Catholic Christendom behind it. Reaction to the bad news as it trickled in took the form of prayers and masses, as if a miracle would be granted if demanded with sufficient passion. Indeed, the English perceived the defeat of the Armada to be a Protestant miracle.

But neither the motive for, nor the defeat of the Spanish expedition of 1588 was entirely religious. Philip at first thought that he had a claim to the English throne, through his second marriage. While he soon recognised that this claim was not practicable, he began to support the ambitions of Mary, Queen of Scots, as soon as the death of her first husband ensured that her accession to the throne of England would not strengthen France. From 1567, when the Scottish Queen arrived in England, Philip was aware of the plots to overthrow Elizabeth in which she was involved. Whether he actively encouraged her treason, or merely hoped to benefit from it, is not clear. Certainly, when she was executed, Mary bequeathed her claim to the English throne to Philip. As well as his hopes of claiming the English throne for himself, or at least for some other Catholic monarch, Philip also needed to prevent the English Queen interfering in his realms. England gave significant help both to the Dutch and to Dom Antonio, the claimant who resisted Philip's hold on Portugal. Elizabeth had also allowed, and indeed encouraged, her men to plunder the Spanish lands in America. The piracy of such men as Hawkins and Drake meant that huge amounts were spent in fortifying the towns of the West Indies, and Drake's circumnavigation in the late 1570s indicated that no part of the Spanish Main was safe from attack. In the end, both Drake and Hawkins were to die in an unsuccessful attack on the West Indies in 1595, but in the decades before they had done considerable harm to Spain's trade and treasure. But even in European waters, Spanish treasure was not safe from England. When treasure ships taking shelter in English ports were impounded in 1568, hostility was bound to grow.

Philip had every reason to be confident that he would defeat the English. After all, dynasties in England had, throughout history, been changed by foreign invasion, most recently in 1485. Philip's ships had been more than equal to theirs in the Azores in 1582–83, and since then he had been building up his navy, not least to ensure that he could continue to control the huge Portuguese empire. While his desperate finances could ill afford the great expense of the Enterprise, victory would solve so many of his problems that it was certainly worth the expenditure. The occupation of England would, at a stroke, settle the revolt in the Netherlands; it would ensure that the Catholics remained dominant in France; it would safeguard Spain's worldwide trade for ever. Much has been written about the defeat of the Spanish Armada. The classic work by Garrett Mattingly[14] explains in detail the tactics which led to English victory, but more recently Geoffrey Parker[15] has argued that Philip's methods and interference meant that the entire plan was unworkable. A plan involving a combined assault by ships from Spain and troops for the Netherlands requires, at the least, modern rapid communications and reliable and trusting liaison between commanders. Despite the terrible losses sustained by the 1588 fleet, Philip could not believe that God had forsaken him: further unsuccessful attempts against England continued until his death in 1598.

Philip always had both secular and religious reasons for his foreign policies. It seems, however, that the conviction that he was doing the will of God may have persuaded him to continue with policies beyond the stage when compromise would have been both wiser and more economically sound. His lack of success, seen by his enemies as proof that God was not on his side, may be more reasonably explained by a consideration of the mismatch between his resources and working methods and the problems which confronted him.

Questions

1. How accurate is it to describe Philip II as the last of the crusading kings?
2. Why, in the reign of Elizabeth, did the Spanish come to replace the French as the greatest foreign threat to the interests of the English nation? (EDEXCEL Summer 1998)

SOURCES

1. PHILIP'S METHODS AND IDEAS

Source A: the Duke of Alba, writing to Philip's secretary, Gabriel Zayas, in February 1573.

I beat my head against the wall when I hear them talk of the cost here! It is not the Turks who are troubling Christendom, but the heretics, and these are already within our gates ... for the love of God, ask for the new supplies that I have detailed to His Majesty, because what is at stake is nothing less than the survival of his states.

Source B: Louis de Requesens describes the Netherlands' situation in January 1575.

I shall say only that matters here are in such a terrible state, and so impossible to sustain, that we have to give in to all they want, so long as religion is excepted. And we will have to act so quickly that there will be no time to consult. . . . I agree that Your Majesty should send someone of the blood royal, remove all foreigners, and restore the old form of government.

Source C: Philip in a letter to Requesens, October 1575.

With such difference of opinions I have found myself very confused. And since I don't know the truth of what is going on there, I neither know the solution that is necessary, nor what to think. It seems to me that the most reliable is to believe neither one side nor the other, since I think that both go to extremes. I think that the best view to take, though with great discretion, is in the middle.

Source D: Philip's draft of an appeal to the Cortes, April 1588.

We must be fully armed and on guard and ready for whatever may happen. This obliges us to make heavy and unprecedented expenditure, or else leave everything to terrible disaster. Nothing less is at stake than the security of our seas and of America and of our fleets, and the security of our own homes. We can go forward only if the Cortes does something to help, for you know the state of the treasury. Confirm to me the confidence that I have in such good subjects. Come forward with the speedy supplies that this moment demands, and discuss the matter with the attention and concern that I very much expect from your loyalty and love for God's service and my own.

Source E: Don Juan de Silva, 1589, comments on the King's work methods.

We have known for years that the detailed attention that His Majesty devotes to the most trifling things is a subject for regret, because when a man finds things to do in order to avoid working, it is what we call a pastime; but when he works in order to find things to do it cannot be given the name it deserves. It is certainly true that His Majesty's brain, although it must be the largest in the world, like that of any other human being, is not capable of organising the multitude of his affairs without making some division between those that he should deal with himself and those that he cannot avoid delegating to others. It s equally true that His Majesty does not make this distinction. . . . Instead, he leaves nothing entirely alone, and takes from everyone the material that should be delegated (concerning individuals and details) and so does not concentrate on the general and the important because he finds them too tiring. . . . Thus no-one takes responsibility for the most important matters pending between His Majesty and his ministers, and everything is decided at random, casting our bread upon the waters but never getting any back. As a result, we spend time and effort in avoiding the measures that are needed, in taking them when we lack time, money and opportunity, in making savings that cost three times more than is saved, in starting in haste because we are late and in starting badly because we are in haste.

Questions

1. Explain the context of Philip's appeal to the Cortes (Source D). (2 marks)
*2. Identify the solutions suggested by Requesens for the Netherlands (Source B) and consider whether they would in fact have solved the problems confronting the province. (3 marks)

3. Discuss and explain the difference in tone between Sources A and B. (5 marks)
4. How far does Source C exemplify the points made in Source E? (6 marks)
5. 'The greatest problem of Philip's foreign policy was the King himself.' How far do these sources confirm or refute this statement? (9 marks)

Worked answer

*2. [It is well worth identifying the three suggestions he makes, and commenting briefly on each in turn.]

The idea of sending someone of royal blood derives from the fact that the Netherlands had, during the reign of Charles, become used to the presence of the King himself, or a member of his family as regent. Indeed, Margaret of Parma had been regent until 1567. Philip himself was aware of this need, and on several occasions implied that he would himself come; in the event, however, he continued to appoint nobles and churchmen, and then to supervise their every move. Removing all foreigners would have reassured the Netherlanders that they were perceived as more than merely an outpost. But Philip needed to be able to communicate with his ministers, and his inability to speak any language but Spanish was almost certainly one of the reasons for his reluctance to trust non-Spaniards. As for restoring the old form of government, this was out of the question. The rebellion and invasions from 1568 on had resulted in the establishment of new tribunals and systems of government, and in determined and brutal military action against the rebel towns. Philip could not have restored the previous system and still have maintained control. Besides, the Dutch were not interested in any settlement in which 'religion is excepted'.

2. PHILIP'S REPUTATION ABROAD

Source F: part of an Edict of the States General of the Netherlands, 1581.

The Prince is created for his subjects (without whom he cannot be a prince) to govern them according to right and reason, and defend and love them as a father does his children and a shepherd does his sheep when he risks his body and life for their safety. It is clear therefore that if he acts differently and instead of protecting his subjects endeavours to oppress and molest them and to deprive them of their ancient liberty, privileges and customs and to command and use them like slaves, he must be regarded not as a prince but as a tyrant. And according to right and reason his subjects, at any rate, must no longer recognise him as a prince ... but should renounce him; in his stead another must be elected to be an overlord called to protect them. This becomes even more true when these subjects have been unable either to soften their Prince's heart through explanations humbly made, or to turn him away from his tyrannical enterprise, and have no other means left to protect their ancient liberty.... And this should happen particularly in these countries, which have always been governed (as they should be) in accordance with the oath taken by the Prince at his inauguration and in conformity with the privileges, customs and old traditions of these countries which he swears to maintain. Moreover, nearly all these countries have accepted their Prince conditionally, by contracts and agreements and if the Prince breaks them he legally forfeits his sovereignty.

Source G: a Dutch view of Philip II's betrayal of Sebastian of Portugal.

Now when King Sebastian was come to the age of four and twenty years, the said King Sebastian at last determined to pass into Africa with a great and puissant army ... and for the better accomplishment thereof he prayed his uncle King Philip of Castile to vouchsafe some aid unto him in that behalf. The King of Castile, granting this petition, promised to aid him with fifty galleys well appointed and furnished and four thousand armed soldiers. King Sebastian, trusting thereunto, with all care and diligence prepared his army, wherewith in the month of June 1578 he departed from Lisbon.... But the King of Castile ... not only denied his promise but also (that is far worse) caused a proclamation to be made ... whereby all his subjects were commanded upon great penalties that none of them should accompany King Sebastian in that voyage, whereof certainly there can no other conjecture be gathered, saving only that the King of Castile, by his unmeasurable ambition and insatiable desire to have dominion, neither coveted nor hoped for any other thing than only that the young Prince King (*sic*) Sebastian his nephew, for want of sufficient force, should be overthrown and come to destruction in the same journey, so as thereupon the said King of Castile might by that mean have opportunity to join the Kingdom of Portugal to his Kingdom of Castile as it came to pass.

Source H: a Dutch rallying call against the machinations of Philip II.

Whosoever therefore shall rightly consider all these dangers and great inconveniences which the said King Don Anthonio hath endured and escaped, may easily judge that all this came not to pass without God's peculiar providence and divine sufferance, and that some great matter of importance is hid thereunder, namely a great hope is to be conceived thereof that almighty God will use the said King Don Antonio as a fit instrument to break the great power and force of the King of Castile, whereby through his excessive and unmeasurable ambition he would else in tract of time invade not only all Christendom but also all the rest of the world . . . to thie intent that upon the subduing of them according to his fantsy he might easily and freely spred his armies over England, Germany, France and other nations . . . for that they receive or at least permit in their countries any other religion than only the Catholic Romish religion. . . . This is the mark he shooteth at and will easily hit except the other Christian princes (before the evil creep any further) have special regard to oppose themselves to his power and force by aiding the provinces united of the low countries now greatly afflicted, and also and that most specially the said King Don Anthonio who with the aid of some reasonable navy of ten or twelve thousand men furnished with victuals, munitions and other necessaries may in short time without any great difficulty recover his Kingdom. . . . Syth therefore it manifestly appeareth by the premises that the said King Don Anthonio hath a rightful and most just cause, it is to be wished that all Christian princes or the most part of them would of their own accord offer themselves to aid and succour him to recover his kingdom, whereof he is unjustly and tyrannously despoiled by the King of Castile. [*The spellings throughout are those of the source.*]

Source I: Philip II's response to Cardinal King Henry of Portugal's establishment of a Council of Judges to decide the accession on his death.

He neither had nor acknowledged any Judge on earth, but only in heaven. And therefore he would not commit his right and title to the determination of any judges who should be appointed concerning this matter, adding withal how he was sufficiently informed by his best learned lawyers in his own kingdom that there was no other personage in the world saving only himself that had lawful right to succeed in the said Kingdom of Portugal . . . which right in case it should be denied him, that then he would obtain the Kingdom by force of arms.

Questions

1. Identify King Sebastian (Source G) and King Don Anthonio (Source H) (2 marks)
2. On what grounds could Philip claim that it was 'only himself that had lawful right' to the throne of Portugal? (2 marks)
*3. Discuss the reasons why the pamphlet from which Sources G and H are taken was published, and sold well, in England. (6 marks)

4. Explain the developments and decisions in the Netherlands which produced the reaction expressed by Source F. (6 marks)
5. Comment on the view that *each* of these sources should be read as propaganda rather than as factual information. (9 marks)

Worked answer

*3. *[It is important to begin by deducing the date of the pamphlet, as credit will be given for this (otherwise the date would have been included in the heading!). This will enable you to be specific in the points you make about English attitudes.]*

This pamphlet appears to have been written between 1580 and 1585. Philip seized the throne of Portugal in 1580, and for some years Don Anthonio actively tried to claim it. From 1585 onwards, however, he was a refugee at the English court, and it was clear that Philip's hold on Portugal was complete. Pamphlets published in the Netherlands were regularly imported into England, using the same routes through which Lollard and Lutheran literature had been brought in earlier years.

English people would be happy to hear unpleasant accusations against the Spanish. Many could still remember the brief government of England by Philip in the 1550s, when Calais was lost by England's involvement in Habsburg wars. Hostility had grown with rumours of Spanish support for the plots of the imprisoned Queen of Scots, and with conflict on the high seas and in the Spanish colonies. Drake had only recently returned from his triumphant circumnavigation of the world previously perceived as a Spanish property.

Protestantism in England had been strengthened, for example, by the excommunication of Elizabeth I in 1571, and Philip was seen as the champion of the 'Romish' Church. Germany, France and the Netherlands had all suffered from the Catholic interference of Philip and his family. Attempts to prevent the growth of Protestantism in Germany, the Spanish approval of the massacre of Protestants in France, and the persecution of the Calvinists of the Netherlands, were all common knowledge, and seen as ominous to an English populace who recalled the martyrs of the reign of Philip and Mary.

Above all, English people would be happy to read that Spain could be defeated 'without any difficulty', as it was clear that the conflict between England and Spain would worsen within the next few years.

8

WAS THE SIXTEENTH CENTURY 'A GOLDEN CENTURY' FOR SPAIN?

BACKGROUND NARRATIVE

Contemporaries certainly saw this as a golden century for Spain. Following the unification of its different kingdoms, Spain came to rule the largest empire the world had ever seen. During the reign of Charles it included much of eastern Europe, although these Habsburg lands were never really a part of the Spanish empire. Philip acquired the last kingdom of the Iberian peninsula with the taking of Portugal in 1580, thus extending his overseas empire to every latitude and longitude known to Europe. All the wealth of the Indies, including gold, poured into the harbours of Iberia, and Spain was the envy of other nations.

A visible expression of this glory was the intellectual 'flowering' of Spain. Just as the Catholic monarchs sponsored the opening of new seats of learning, and of new editions of the bible, so Charles and Philip were patrons of scholarship and of the arts, Philip in his turn sponsoring a new polyglot bible. At the same time, architecture flourished, with new palaces and administrative offices expressing the austere grandeur of Spain's international status. Artists of international repute found employment in Spain under both Charles and Philip. In religion, too, Spain dominated European, or at least Catholic, thought. Two of the great saints of the period, Teresa of Avila and Ignatius Loyola, were Spanish, and devotional works of an enduring type were printed in Spain. Indeed, Philip is said to have read little else – aside, of course, from state papers.

Until the 1570s, Spain's armies and navies were the envy of Europe, and were seen as invincible. But all these developments and triumphs came at a cost to the ordinary people of Spain. The great empire of Charles V meant that Castilians had to accept the rule of regents rather than of their monarch in person; and while Philip remained with them, his working methods increasingly cut him off from the people. The royal tax collectors, however, were a constant presence, and the burden of taxation grew throughout the century, from the moment when rebellion in Ghent convinced Charles that it would be less painful to collect revenue from his people in Castile. The possession of the empire in America, and subsequently in Asia, increased the burden of defence, and the alienation of two of the main maritime peoples of Europe, the Dutch and the English, made Spanish colonies much more vulnerable than they had been when the main enemy was France. The empire also distorted the economy of Spain, by accelerating and worsening inflation.

Centralisation reduced the influence of the citizens over their own affairs and, ironically, the mechanisms established by Ferdinand and Isabella to reduce the power of the nobility, such as the system of *corregidors*, increasingly fell back into noble hands. Although the Cortes of Castile continued to meet, at most sessions its grievances were ignored although it still voted the required taxes.

While literature and, particularly, art, continued to flourish, Spain in the seventeenth century lost much of its international influence. With the renewed dominance of France under the Bourbons, Philip III and Philip IV ceased to play the major part that their predecessors had done in the affairs of Europe. And the growing strength of England and the Netherlands soon ensured that the net costs of defending the empire were greater than its revenues. The fact that Portugal regained its independence less than half-a-century after the death of Philip II is an indication of this decline. The two analyses which follow consider the cultural developments which have given the title 'the golden century' to this period in Spanish history, and provide a summary of the economic and political state of Spain at its end.

ANALYSIS (1): IS IT TRUE THAT THE SIXTEENTH CENTURY SAW 'A REMARKABLE FLOWERING OF ART AND LITERATURE IN SPAIN'?

The reign of Ferdinand and Isabella was one of considerable intellectual development for Spain, encouraged by the union of the two crowns and the ending of the *reconquista*. The peninsula was at peace for most of their reign, and Isabella in particular encouraged artists and scholars. Printing presses were established in both Castile and Aragon, and the reforms put in place in government meant that education was the best route into the administration. The reliance of the Catholic monarchs on *letrados*, those with legal training, set education at a premium. Young nobles, too, recognised the need for good Latin, as the military arts were increasingly reserved for paid professionals. Isabella invited the scholar and historian Peter Martyr to visit Spain, and is said to have read his works. The founding of new universities at Alcalá (1508) and Cuenca (1510) is a measure of the importance attached to education at the higher level. At the village level, education was a matter for the parish priests, and the reforms put in place by Cisneros improved their commitment and standing.

Charles I, in his turn, actively promoted the development of the universities in Spain, attending in person the lectures of Vitoria and taking a close interest in the cultural artefacts of the New World as they were brought to him. The growth of heresy in other parts of his empire, however, caused Charles V to look anxiously at foreign intellectual influences, and in 1533 several prominent Erasmians were forced to abjure their views. Many of the pictograph books of the Aztecs were destroyed as heathen works, although some of the feather regalia of Montezuma and his nobility are still preserved in Charles' eastern capital Vienna. To modern eyes, possibly the greatest vandalism of the century was the melting down of the golden art works which composed much of the ransom unsuccessfully offered for the life of the Inca warlord Atahuallpa. At the time, however, these were expressions of a heathen idolatry and so had to be converted into neutral ingots.[1]

The Holy Office of the Inquisition was in effect a 'gigantic teaching machine',[2] as we saw in Chapter 6. Defendants before the Tribunal at Cuenca demonstrate the work of the Inquisition. Between 1564–80, only 33 per cent of those questioned said they had confessed annually to a priest; during the next twenty years, that figure doubled to 66 per cent.[3] Spain took the lead in the Counter-Reformation across Europe, and Spanish bishops played a major part in the Council of Trent. Just as Ferdinand and Isabella had sponsored a polyglot edition of the bible, so

Philip authorised a new Latin translation of the scriptures for the new Antwerp bible of 1568–72. Although Philip himself (when not busy with paperwork) rarely read anything other than devotional works such as those by St Teresa of Avila, nevertheless the library at the Escorial contained large numbers of writings of all kinds, including Islamic manuscripts and heretical writings. The most important writer in Spain, Miguel de Cervantes, was rewarded for his early works (such as his pastoral romance *Galatea*) by his appointment as tax collector in Granada. It was not till the start of the next century that his greatest work, *Don Quixote*, was written. It is doubtful whether Philip would have enjoyed its irreverent attitude to the great chivalric traditions of the peninsula, since, during his reign, Spain was gradually cutting itself off from the academic influences of the rest of Europe. Although Philip appointed humanist tutors for his son Don Carlos from 1559, the Papal Index of Prohibited Books was applied in Spain, and Castilians were prohibited from studying at foreign universities. The great *autos de fé* in Valladolid and Seville in 1559, which targeted Protestants, demonstrated the direction the King wished the intellectual life of Spain to take.

Architecture was less likely to be controversial, and the sixteenth century saw a tremendous amount of royal and noble building. The monarchs were happy to have the nobility spending their time and money on palaces rather than insurrections. During the century the Isabelline style (a kind of Flemish gothic), gave way to a more classical and Renaissance style. Charles had little time to spare, but did commission new government buildings such as the *Chancellería* in Valladolid, and ordered the building of the cathedral within the Great Mosque of Córdoba. He also began the palace at the Alhambra in Granada. In comparison, however, Philip achieved much more as a builder. In 1578 he approved the plans for new buildings for the state archive in Simancas, and throughout his reign he built new, and improved old, royal palaces. Charles had ordered a new palace on the site of the hunting lodge at El Pardo, but it was Philip who had seen to the detail of the building, and this appears to have been the start of his obsession. He employed the architects Juan Bautista de Toledo (1562–67) Juan de Herrera (1567–85) and they enthusiastically implemented his ideas of combined austerity and grandeur. Philip's greatest achievement in building was the Escorial, constructed between 1563 and 1585 and dedicated to St Lawrence, on whose feast day, August 10, in 1557 Philip had defeated the King of France at St Quentin. The palace–monastery was, however, only one of more than ten royal palaces built or improved at Philip's orders. 'Thousands of workers were employed for decades, and immense quantities of materials were transported into and across the peninsula.'[4]

This expenditure continued throughout the reign, regardless of other calls on the overstretched revenues of Spain.

The palaces were embellished with the best that the period could offer. Although he usually dressed in black, Philip's clothes were always sumptuous, and his third wife, Elizabeth of Valois, was said 'never to wear the same dress twice'. Whether this is true or not, she did spend 10,000 ducats on jewels alone in the years 1562–65. Philip appointed the composer and musician Tomas Luis de Victoria to the Royal Chapel. He purchased works by Hieronymus Bosch and Van der Weyden, which hung in his private apartments, and he commissioned many works by Titian. The Spanish portrait painters Alonso Sanchez Coello and Juan Pantoja de la Cruz enjoyed his patronage, but the greatest of the Spanish painters of the period, was less fortunate. Near the beginning of his career, El Greco was commissioned to paint for the King. *The Dream of Philip II* (1578) and *The Martyrdom of St Maurice* (1582) were duly delivered, but after that Philip did not use the artist. It is not clear whether he simply did not like the elongated shapes and tormented faces of El Greco's saints and churchmen, or whether he regarded them as insufficiently orthodox. His successors were to prefer the courtly portraiture of Velázsquez, but were to continue the royal patronage of artists.

Philip did not neglect the more scientific aspects of knowledge. He commissioned and purchased maps of his possessions in Europe and America, and these were displayed on the walls of his apartments. During the 1560s, sketches of Spanish towns were drawn for him by Anton van der Wyngaerde, and Philip also had 'Topographical Relations' written of Spain and the Indies during the 1570s, detailing all kinds of information about geography, history and folklore.

It is unnecessary to point out that any 'golden age' is bound to be instigated and enjoyed by the rich elite classes alone. Nevertheless, the cultural glories enjoyed by visitors to Spain today are in large measure the product of movements which began in the sixteenth century, and as such cannot be dismissed merely as the hobbies of the court circle. The extent to which the population as a whole may be said to have benefited from these three reigns is considered next.

Question

'Philip II's reign should be remembered as "the Golden Age of Spain", not as some prelude to Spanish decline.' Discuss this comment on Spain in the period to 1598. (EDEXCEL Summer 1998)

ANALYSIS (2): DID PHILIP II LEAVE SPAIN WEAKER OR STRONGER THAN IT WAS AT THE START OF THE CENTURY?

Philip was able to increase the size of his empire; the annexation of Portugal and its great Asian and African empire certainly led contemporaries to perceive Spain as a great nation. The loss of the northern Netherlands, although inevitable, was not complete before his death, and although Spain had been defeated in its invasion attempt, the war against England also continued beyond Philip's reign. Thus it was possible to claim for Spain as great a strength in foreign policy terms as it had in 1559. On the other hand, Spain's international status had suffered from failures in Europe. The great triumph against the Turks was more than balanced by the defeat of the Armada, and the endless struggle against the Dutch. Spain was slow to adapt to its maritime role, or to adopt the new methods of sea warfare. Not until the 1590s did Spanish naval designers begin to emulate the methods of their enemies: Spanish ships continued to expect to close and board, although the Armada made clear that artillery battles at gunshot distance were the way of the future. Not even the acquisition of the Portuguese navy enabled Spain to achieve full command of the sea. While this may be explained in part by the shortage of timber in Spain, it also indicates a lack of determined long-term policy making. The huge costs of an international empire were recognised, but there was no choice, as Don Luis de Requesens recognised as early as 1565:

> It may be that there are old men in Castile who believe that we were better off when we held no more than that realm . . . and in truth if they could [would] return . . . to that time when there was a King in Aragon and another in Naples and a lord in Flanders and another in Burgundy and a Duke in Milan, and would likewise distribute what the King of France has now joined together; but supposing that the world, or at least Christendom, did come to be reduced into only the power of His Majesty and of the King of France, and what is ours could not be otherwise unless it belonged to our enemy, it [would still be] necessary to conserve [what we have].[5]

At home in Spain, issues was equally complex. The Castilians had their wish, namely their King living among them; but dynastic security was denied them. Despite his four marriages, and his numerous children, the succession was not assured. The death of his heir in 1568 was as much a relief as a tragedy. Professor Geoffrey Parker calls Don Carlos 'unpredictable and unlovable',[6] but also points out that his health and mental problems may be explained genetically: Don Carlos had only four great-grandparents rather than eight. Of the four sons born to Philip and his cousin Anne of Austria in the 1570s, only one survived into the 1580s. The Castilians also found that their King was not often seen among them, as had been traditional. The workload of a huge empire mounted up as a consequence of Philip's inability to delegate, and he toiled day and night through mountains of paper. His government was both reluctant to and incapable of making major decisions fast; Philip's need to read and ponder the views of all before reaching and transmitting his conclusions was bound to have an enervating effect on all aspects of government. And when he had spare time, he spent it hunting, or planning and supervising new building works, rather than travelling among his people. In the last years of his reign, his isolation was exacerbated by crippling and painful illness.

Natural catastrophes may well have added to the serious problems which confronted Spain. Climate change made worse the crisis in foodstuffs which arose in overpopulated areas. It is striking that Spain did not industrialise as rapidly as did other countries of western Europe, for example in metal production. The building of the royal palaces illustrates this clearly: naturally, marble would have been imported from Italy: but it is extraordinary to see that the nails used in the building were imported as well. Although Spain produced some of the best wool in Europe – and, indeed, the agriculture of the peninsula had been distorted earlier in the century by the added privileges given to the *Mesta* – almost all textile production had migrated from Spain to the Netherlands and to Italy. Thus the voracious markets of the New World were being fed by the industries even of Spain's enemies, including England, rather than by the domestic producers.

The benefits of *hidalguía* were well known to the Spanish, and throughout the century families aspired to achieve it. The *hidalgo* class was exempt from some taxes, and was entitled to honorific and cere-monial privileges. Thus enterprising people who had made profits in trade or commerce would purchase the right for their families to live as gentlemen, and their entrepreneurial skills would fall into abeyance. Meanwhile, the poor were taxed, and the low yield of taxation made the crown the more willing to sell titles, annuities and offices. It seems probable that men of vision and determination preferred to seek their fortunes in the empire abroad, and the drain of young males from Spain, referred to in Chapter 6, inevitably weakened the country at a time when other economies in Europe were forced to evolve to cope with population pressure on resources.

The great wealth of the Indies was also a problem for Spain. It seems probable that the supposed riches flowing into Spain encouraged the extravagant foreign policy pursued by both Charles and Philip. Certainly, they continued to rely on borrowing despite the near bankruptcies of Charles' reign and the four actual bankruptcies of 1557, 1560, 1575 and 1596. Most of Philip's and Charles' wars ended in negotiated settlements of one kind or another; but they were allowed to drag on for many years before arrangements were made which could have been made at the start of the conflict. A further proof that large imports of silver did not in themselves constitute wealth came from the constant shortage of coin in Spain. The English financier of the period, Thomas Gresham, had coined the law that 'bad money drives out good', and this was proved in Spain, where foreign merchants, sailors and mercenaries all preferred to take their pay in good coin than in other commodities, and the silver specie left Spain at a tremendous rate. The regular debasements also meant that bankers were reluctant to invest directly in Spain, and insisted on taking their interest payments directly from the treasure fleets.

Debased coins had an accelerating effect on the inflation which had begun with a shortage of commodities and excess money earlier in the century. Prices did not begin to stabilise until near the end of the century; while those paying money rents may have benefited, for most the rising prices made daily life more difficult. For the government, it multiplied the problems of finding sufficient revenue. Each time the Cortes was asked for additional funds there were protests, with a near refusal in 1575. Only the Castilian Cortes was sufficiently biddable to produce additional taxes, and by the end of the reign their patience was exhausted. In 1598 they demanded not only an end to the *millones*, but also a reduction in the amount of the *alcabalá*.

The two serious rebellions of Philip's reign had specific political and religious rather than economic causes. Nevertheless they are a measure of the discontent which had not been expressed in Spain since the early 1520s. Even victories abroad were no compensation for heavy taxation and commodity shortages at home; and as victories were replaced by defeats, discontent in Aragon erupted into open rebellion, which took some time to quell.

It seems certain, then, that the Spain which Philip left to his son was weaker than the one he himself had inherited. Both the royal finances and the underlying economy had been distorted by his policies, and damage had been done which was irreparable. The confidence of the Spanish had been shaken by defeats and territorial loss, and, while more than two centuries were to pass before Spain lost its overseas empire, it would never again play the leading role in Europe to which it had been accustomed. The fact that Portugal was able to win its independence war in 1640 was a measure of Spain's growing weakness.

Question

How serious a problem was inflation in sixteenth century Spain?

SOURCES

1. THE CULTURAL LIFE OF SIXTEENTH-CENTURY SPAIN

Source A: extract from *The Life of St Teresa of Avila*, 1565.

On St Clare's Day, as I was going to Communion, that saint appeared to me and told me to take courage. She promised that she would help me if I went forward with what I had begun. I conceived a great devotion for her and she has truly kept her word. For a Convent of her order, which is close to ours, is at present helping to maintain us. What is more, she has gradually brought this plan of mine to such perfection that the same Rule of poverty which obtains in her house is also observed in ours, and we live on alms. It was essential to get the Holy Father's approval for our existing without any revenue, and the procuring of that cost me no small labour. But the Lord is doing even greater things for us and it may be at the request of this blessed saint that he is doing them. Without any demand on our part, His Majesty is providing most amply for our needs.

Source B: an extract for the poem *From Life to Heaven*, by Luis de Leon, 1577.

Crowned in flowering snow
and purple, the Good Shepherd moves his dear flock
to sweet pastures that grow
in you, and he can walk
about with no need for sling, staff or crook.

Leading the way he goes
followed by his happy sheep; these he feeds
with the immortal rose:
a flower that blooms and needs
only to be enjoyed to make more seeds.

And now into the mountain
of perfect goodness, leading them ahead,
he bathes them in the fountain
of all joy. Food is spread
by him the pastor, pasture on which we're fed.

Source C: from *The Adventures of Don Quixote*, Miguel de Cervantes (1547–1616).

The reader must know, then, that this gentleman, in the times when he had nothing to do – as was the case for most of the year – gave himself up to the reading of books of sources: and enjoyed so much that he almost entirely forgot his hunting and even the care of his estate. So old and foolish, indeed, did he grow on this subject that he sold many acres of corn-land to buy these books of chivalry to read, and in this way brought home every one he could get.... These writings drove the poor knight out of his wits; and he passed sleepless nights trying to understand them and disentangle their meaning; though Aristotle himself would never have unravelled or understood them, even if he had been resurrected for that sole purpose.... In short, he so buried himself in his books that he spent the nights reading from twilight till daybreak, and the days from dawn till dark, and so from little sleeping and much reading, his brain dried up and he lost his wits.

Source D: from a questionnaire on the Spanish American Empire, to be filled in by provincial governors and magistrates, 1577.

Question 17. State whether the town is situated in a healthful or unhealthful place and, if unhealthful, the cause for this if it can be learned; note the kinds of illness that are prevalent and the remedies employed for curing them.

Question 18. State how far or how close is any nearby remarkable mountain or mountain range, in what direction it lies, and what it is called.

...

Question 20. Mention the important lakes, lagoons and fountains within the bounds of the towns, and any notable things about them there may be.

Question 21. Mention volcanoes, caves, and all other remarkable and admirable works of nature there may be in the district which are worthy of being known.

...

Question 28. Describe the gold and silver mines, and other veins of metals or minerals and mineral dyes there may be in the district and within the confines of the town.

Question 29. State the deposits of precious stones, jasper, marble and other important and esteemed materials which likewise may exist.

Source E: *The Tribute Money*, by Titian, © National Gallery London

Questions

1. What evidence is there in Source D that the interest of the Spanish government concerning America extended beyond economic issues? (3 marks)
2. What do Sources A and B tell us about the importance of religion to the cultural life of Philip II's Spain? (4 marks)
3. Study the two pictures reproduced as Source E. What light do they throw on the fact that Titian was patronised by Philip II but El Greco was not? (6 marks)

*4. What aspects of Spanish life are being satirised by Cervantes in Source C? (5 marks)

5. Is it accurate to conclude from these sources that the main focus of the cultural life of Spain in the later sixteenth century was literary rather than artistic? (7 marks)

Worked answer

*4. *[For five marks, it is important to make several points, and to expand upon them.]*

When Miguel de Cervantes wrote his famous novel, he was aware of the undue influence which stories of chivalry had in the education of all ranks of Spanish nobility, and this was his first target. Stories of the heroes of the *reconquista* were used to inculcate notions of heroism and bravery; but even more popular were the adventures of Amadis of Gaul. *Conquistadores* like Bernal Díaz referred to this Arthurian hero as a yardstick for their own achievements. But Cervantes is also satirising the impoverishment of the landed nobility, who continued to focus on their lineage while their peasants suffered and their lands fell into disrepair. The suggestion that for most of the year he had nothing to do reinforces the view that the landowners were insufficiently involved in the working of the estates. The reference to Aristotle implies that the nobility regarded these stories of chivalry as being of intellectual value, though the suggestion that excessive reading might dry up the brain appears to be a comment on all forms of education.

2. PROBLEMS FOR THE PEOPLE OF SPAIN

Source F: Tomas de Mercado writes about the silver of the Indies, 1569.

In Spain, the very source and found of escudos and crowns, scarcely a handful can be scraped together, whereas, if you go to Genoa, Rome, Antwerp or Venice, you will see in the streets of the bankers and money changers, without exaggeration, as many piles of coins, minted in Seville, as there are piles of melons in San Salvador.

Source G: Castillo de Bobadilla comments on feudal demands, 1597.

This burden of lodging and clothing and suchlike which a seigneur lays on his vassals, asking them for gifts when they or their children marry, or at Christmas, and that they bake their bread in his ovens or grind their flour in his mills, that they plough his fields and give him carts to carry wood and building materials, or to move house ... all these are odious burdens and must be cut back.

Source H: comparison of some Castilian revenues (ducats) in the 1530s and in the 1590s

	1530s	*1590s*
Alcabalá	267,000	2,800,000
Other tax income from Spain	200,000	5,000,000
Silver from the Indies	375,000	2,000,000

Source I: war in the reigns of Ferdinand and Isabella, Charles I and Philip II (see table opposite)

The darker shading shows decades mainly or mostly occupied by conflict; the pale shading shows decades where some years were occupied by conflict.

Questions

1. Explain the term '*alcabalá*' (source H) What other taxes were the people of Castile required to pay? (3 marks)
2. For what reasons did the four foreign towns mentioned in Source F have large amounts of Spanish specie? (3 marks)
3. Comment on the usefulness of statistics such as those in Source H to a historian. (4 marks)
4. Study the table of wars (Source I). Which of these wars was most likely to affect the ordinary people of Spain and why? (6 marks)
*5. How complete a picture of the problems confronting the people of Spain is provided by these sources? (9 marks)

Worked answer

*5. The shortage of coins in Spain was a great inconvenience for the populace, but this source does not explain the causes of the shortage. Inflation had been a problem for Spain for much of the century, and this had adversely affected communities on fixed incomes, and had destabilised industrial production. Inflation also exacerbated the problems of feudal peasants, as described in Source G, since seigneurs, finding cash payments declining in value, reverted to the more traditional payments in labour and in kind.

Table 8.1 Wars, 1474–1598

	Portugal	Granada	France	Mediterranean and Turks	England	Netherlands	Rebellions in Iberia
1470s	■						
1480s		■					
1490s		▨	■				
1500s			▨	▨			
1510s			▨				
1520s			■	▨		▨	▨
1530s			■	▨			
1540s			■				
1550s				■		▨	
1560s		▨		■		▨	
1570s		▨		■			
1580s	▨				■	■	
1590s					■	■	▨

The huge increase in the revenues of Castile is partly explained by inflation. But at the same time Source H reveals the growing burden of taxation upon the people of Castile; during the 1530s, the Netherlands were bearing perhaps more than their share of the cost of empire, whereas by the last years of the reign of Philip, the burden fell on Spain; indeed, because of the constitutional privileges of the kingdom of Aragon, it fell on the tax payers of Castile. What is not clear from this table is which of the Castilian population actually paid the taxes. Nobles of all ranks were exempt from many taxes, as was the wealth of the Church and some towns. Thus the bulk of taxation was payable by the poorest classes.

The table of wars (Source I) helps to explain why the Spanish were so heavily taxed; it also demonstrates the pressure on the armies of Spain. Young men who joined the armies of Spain found themselves fighting far from home; they were also frequently reduced to mutinying in order to force some payment of back wages. War also, of course, affected trade routes and thus damaged the commerce and industry of Spain.

These sources do not, however, mention other economic difficulties confronting the population of Spain: the increasing urbanisation, in towns like Madrid and Seville, led to squalid conditions, recognised by the new religious orders established to minister to the poor. In addition, the religious pressures on anyone who questioned the church affected not only people of Christian origin but the communities whose forebears had converted from Islam or Judaism. The Inquisition's influence extended to all aspects of life.

As in all countries of Europe at the time, the government of Spain was not a matter of close interest to the mass of the people, particularly since successive rulers summoned the Cortes less frequently. But they were aware of the absence of Charles, and of the isolation of Philip, and this was against the traditions of Castile. This added to all the other miseries of the people of Spain.

NOTES

1. SPAIN AT THE TIME OF ITS 'UNIFICATION'

1 B. Keen and J. H. Mariejol (trans. and ed.): *The Spain of Ferdinand and Isabella* (New Jersey 1961), p. 117.
2 Geoffrey Woodward: *Spain in the Reigns of Ferdinand and Isabella* (London 1997), p. 7.
3 D. W. Lomax: *The Reconquest of Spain* (London 1978).
4 Quoted in J. H. Parry: *Spanish Seaborne Empire* (London 1969).
Source A: *Calendar of Letters, Despatches and State Papers Relating to the Negotiations between England and Spain*, Vol. 1: *1485–1509*, ed. G. A. Bergenroth (London 1862), p. 169.
Source B: Francesco Guicciardini: 'Relazione de Spagna' (1512) quoted in Carlo M. Cipolla: *Before the Industrial Revolution* (London 1976), p. 250.
Source C: quoted in J. H. Elliott: *Imperial Spain* (London 1968), p. 12.
Source D: Pulgar: quoted in Geoffrey Woodward: *Spain in the Reigns of Ferdinand and Isabella* (London 1997), p. 26.
Source E: *Calendar of Letters, Despatches and State Papers Relating to the Negotiations between England and Spain*, Vol. 1: *1485–1509*, ed. G. A. Bergenroth (London 1862), p. 8.

2. THE DOMESTIC POLICIES OF FERDINAND AND ISABELLA

1 Marvin Lunenfeld: *Keepers of the City. The Corregidors of Isabella I of Castile 1474–1504* (Cambridge 1987), p. 72.
2 Marvin Lunenfeld: ibid., p. 74.
3 Stephen Haliczer: *The Communeros of Castile: The Forging of a Revolution 1475–1521* (Wisconsin 1981), p. 29.
4 Quoted in S. W. Baron: *A Social and Religious History of the Jews* (New York 1962 onwards), Vol. XIII pp. 21–2.

Source A: quoted in Geoffrey Woodward: *Spain in the Reigns of Ferdinand and Isabella* (London 1997), pp. 28–9.

Source B: quoted in Geoffrey Woodward: ibid., p. 31.

Source C: from *The Prince* [1513], ed. G. Bull (London 1981), pp. 119–20.

Source D: *Calendar of Letters, Despatches and State Papers Relating to the Negotiations between England and Spain*, Vol 1: *1485–1509*, ed. G. A. Bergenroth (London 1862), p. 76.

Source E: quoted in David Englander, Diana Norman, Rosemary O'Day and W. R. Owens: *Culture and Belief in Europe 1450–1600* (Oxford 1990), pp. 298–9.

Source F: quoted in Geoffrey Woodward: *Spain in the Reigns of Ferdinand and Isabella* (London 1997), p. 76.

Source G: taken from the so-called 'Copy of a letter of the king of Portugal, sent to the King of Castile' ([1505], trans. John Parker, Univ Minnesota Press 1955), p. 13.

Source H: *Calendar of Letters, Despatches and State Papers Relating to the Negotiations between England and Spain*, Vol. 1: *1485–1509*, ed. G. A. Bergenroth (London 1862), p. 51.

3. HOW SUCCESSFUL WERE THE FOREIGN POLICIES OF FERDINAND AND ISABELLA?

1 Felipe Fernandez-Armesto: *Ferdinand and Isabella* (New York 1975), p. 186.

2 G. Woodward: *Spain in the Reigns of Ferdinand and Isabella* (London 1997), p. 89.

3 Quoted in G. Woodward: ibid., p. 90.

Source A: *Calendar of Letters, Despatches and State Papers Relating to the Negotiations between England and Spain*, Vol. 1: *1485–1509*, ed. G. A. Bergenroth (London 1862), p. 135.

Source B: ibid., p. 182.

Source C: ibid., p. 5.

Source D: ibid., pp. 17–18.

Source E: ibid., p. 26.

Source F: taken from the so-called 'Copy of a letter of the king of Portugal, sent to the King of Castile' ([1505] trans. John Parker, Univ Minnesota Press 1955) p. 17.

Source G: quoted in Geoffrey Woodward: *Spain in the Reigns of Ferdinand and Isabella* (London 1997), p. 106.

Source H: Hernando Columbus: *The Life of Columbus*, in *The Four Voyages of Christopher Columbus* (London 1963), p. 37.

Source I: ibid., p. 102.

4. CHARLES I AS RULER OF SPAIN

1 K. Brandi: *The Emperor Charles V*, trans. C. V. Wedgwood (London 1939).
2 J. Alden Mason: *The Ancient Civilisations of Peru* (London 1969), p. 137.
3 S. K. Lothrop: *Inca Treasure as Depicted by Spanish Historians* (Los Angeles 1938) quoted in J. Alden Mason: ibid.
4 Stephen Haliczer: *The Communeros of Castile: The Forging of a Revolution 1475–1521* (Wisconsin 1981).
5 Henry Kamen: *Spain 1469–1716: A Society in Conflict* (London 1983).
6 J. Vicens Vives: *Economic History of Spain* (Barcelona 1959), p. 84.
7 James Casey: *Early Modern Spain: A Social History* (London 1999), ch. 4.
8 ibid., p. 21.
9 C. R. Phillips and W. D. Phillips: *Spain's Golden Fleece: Wool Production and the Wool Trade from the Middle Ages to the Nineteenth Century* (Baltimore MD 1997), p. 294.
Source A: quoted in Stephen Haliczer: *The Communeros of Castile: The Forging of a Revolution 1475–1521* (Wisconsin 1981), p. 165.
Source B: quoted in ibid., p. 165.
Source C: quoted in G. Griffiths: *Representative Government in Western Europe in the 16th Century* (Oxford 1968), p. 41.
Source D: quoted in Stewart Macdonald: *Charles V* (London 1992), p. 27.
Source E: quoted in ibid., p. 34.
Source F: quoted in Stephen Haliczer: op. cit., p. 123.
Source G: Francisco Lopez de Gómara: *Annals of the Emperor Charles V* (trans. R. B. Merriman), quoted in Martyn Rady: *The Emperor Charles V* (London 1988), p. 102.
Source H: J. S. Brewer: *Letters and Papers of the Reign of Henry VIII* (London 1867), p. 317.
Source I: ibid., p. 358.
Source J: quoted in Martyn Rady: *The Emperor Charles V* (London 1988), pp. 104–5.

5. FOREIGN AFFAIRS DURING THE REIGN OF CHARLES I

1 Desmond Seward: *Prince of the Renaissance* (London 1974), p. 147.
2 Martyn Rady: *The Emperor Charles V* (London 1988), pp. 47–8.
3 Quoted in Desmond Seward: op. cit., p. 148.

4 Stewart Macdonald: *Charles V* (London 1992), p. 27.

5 Elsa Strietman in R. Porter and M. Teich (eds): *The Renaissance in National Context* (Cambridge 1992), p. 72.

Source A: quoted in J. S. Brewer: *Letters and Papers of the Reign of Henry VIII* (London 1867), p. 620–1.

Source B: quoted in Desmond Seward: op. cit., p. 136.

Source C: J. S. Brewer: op. cit., pp. 941–2.

Source D: ibid., p. 1458.

Source E: quoted in *English Historical Documents 1485–1558* (ed. C. H. Williams, London 1967), pp. 208–9.

Source F: quoted in Martyn Rady: op. cit., pp. 104–5.

Source G: J. S. Brewer: op. cit., (London 1867) p. 922.

Source H: quoted in Martyn Rady: op. cit., p. 110.

Source I: quoted in Stewart Macdonald: op. cit., p. 94.

Source J: quoted in Martyn Rady: op. cit., p. 112.

6. WHAT PROBLEMS CONFRONTED PHILIP II IN HIS GOVERNMENT OF SPAIN?

1 Henry Kamen: *Philip of Spain* (London 1997).

2 Henry Kamen: ibid., p. 203.

3 Quoted in James Casey: 'Philip II: The Prudent King', *The Historian*, no. 56 (Historical Association, London 1997).

4 James Casey: *Early Modern Spain: A Social History* (London 1999), p. 225.

5 Henry Kamen: op. cit., p. 131.

6 James Casey: op. cit., p. 225.

7 William Monter: *Frontiers of Heresy: The Spanish Inquisition from the Basque Lands to Sicily* (Cambridge: 1990), p. 85.

8 Helen Rawlings: 'The Holy Office of the Inquisition in Spain', *The Historian*, no. 56 (Historical Association, London 1997), p. 33.

9 J. P. Dedieu: 'Christianisation in New Castile', in A. J. Cruz and M. E. Perry (eds) *Culture and Control in Counter Reformation Spain* (Minneapolis 1992), pp. 1–24.

10 James Casey: 'Philip II: The Prudent King', *The Historian*, no. 56 (Historical Association, London 1997).

11 Derived from data in E. J. Hamilton: *American Treasure and the Price Revolution in Spain 1501–1650* (Cambridge MA 1934).

12 Henry Kamen: op. cit., p. 158.

13 James Casey: *Early Modern Spain: A Social History* (London 1999), p. 25.

14 Derived from data in E. J. Hamilton: op. cit.

15 Anthony Peaker: 'New Found Wealth and Economic Decline in Sixteenth Century Spain', *Economics Review* (Summer 1982).

Source A: quoted in Henry Kamen: *Philip of Spain* (New Haven CT and London 1997), p. 76.

Source B: quoted in ibid., p. 100.

Source C: quoted in Fernand Braudel: *The Mediterranean and the Mediterranean World in the Age of Philip II*, Vol. II (London 1978), p. 965.

Source D: quoted in James Casey: 'Philip II of Spain: The Prudent King', *The Historian*, no. 56 (Historical Association, London 1997).

Source E: quoted in David Englander, Diana Norman, Rosemary O'Day and W. R. Owens: *Culture and Belief in Europe 1450–1600* (Oxford 1990), pp. 301–2.

Source F: from *Explanation of the True and Lawful Right and title of the most Excellent Prince Anthonie* (Leyden, Christopher Plantyn's Printing House 1585; published under licence from Maurice, Earl of Nassau), pp. 2–3.

Source G: quoted in Henry Kamen: op. cit., pp. 157–8.

Source H: quoted in Henry Kamen: op. cit., pp. 286–7.

Source I: quoted in Henry Kamen: op. cit., p. 293.

7. THE SUCCESSES AND FAILURES OF PHILIP II's FOREIGN POLICY

1 F. Braudel: *The Mediterranean and the Mediterranean World in the Age of Philip II* (London 1972), p. 676.

2 Geoffrey Parker: *The Grand Strategy of Philip II* (London 1998), p. 283.

3 Henry Kamen: *Philip of Spain* (New Haven CT and London 1997), p. 320.

4 J. L. Motley: *The Rise of the Dutch Republic* (London 1856).

5 Quoted in James Casey: 'Philip II of Spain: The Prudent King', *The Historian* no. 56 (Historical Association, London 1997).

6 Geoffrey Parker: op. cit.

7 F. Braudel: op. cit., p. 374.

8 Geoffrey Parker, op cit., p. 140.

9 quoted in James Casey: op. cit.

10 Henry Kamen: op. cit., p. 255.

11 Geoffrey Parker: op. cit., pp. 134–5.

12 R. A. Stradling: *The Armada of Flanders* (Cambridge 1992), opening chapters

13 Quoted in Geoffrey Parker: op. cit., p. 105.

14 Garrett Mattingly: *The Defeat of the Spanish Armada* (London 1962).

15 Geoffrey Parker: op. cit.

Source A: quoted in Henry Kamen: *Philip of Spain* (New Haven CT and London 1997), p. 146.

Source B: quoted in Henry Kamen: ibid., p. 155.

Source C: quoted in Henry Kamen: ibid., p. 147.

Source D: quoted in Henry Kamen: ibid., p. 274.

Source E: quoted in Geoffrey Parker: *The Grand Strategy of Philip II* (New Haven CT and London 1998), pp. 66–7.

Source F: quoted by Elsa Strietman in R. Porter and M. Teich (eds): *The Renaissance in National Context* (Cambridge 1992), p. 75.

Sources G, H and I: from *Explanation of the True and Lawful Right and title of the most Excellent Prince Anthonie* (Leyden, Christopher Plantyn's Printing House 1585; published under licence from Maurice, Earl of Nassau), pp. 3–4; 53–4, 56; 9.

8. WAS THE SIXTEENTH CENTURY 'A GOLDEN CENTURY' FOR SPAIN?

1 For examples of the few golden artworks which survive see, for example, J. Alden Mason: *The Ancient Civilisations of Peru* (London 1957), plates 42–6.

2 J. P. Dedieu: 'Christianisation in New Castile', in A. J. Cruz and M. E. Perry (eds): *Culture and Control in Counter Reformation Spain* (Minneapolis 1992), p. 1.

3 Sara Nalle: *God in La Mancha* (London and Baltimore MD 1992), p. 54.

4 Henry Kamen: *Philip of Spain* (New Haven CT and London 1997), p. 185.

5 Quoted in Geoffrey Parker: *The Grand Strategy of Philip II* (London 1998), p. 284.

6 G. Parker: ibid., p. 119.

Source A: *The Life of St Teresa of Avila* (trans. J. M. Cohen, London 1957), p. 263.

Source B: quoted in David Englander, Diana Norman, Rosemary O'Day and W. R. Owens: *Culture and Belief in Europe 1450–1600* (Oxford 1990), p. 257.

Source C: Miguel de Cervantes: *The Adventures of Don Quixote* (trans. J. M. Cohen, London 1950), p. 32.

Source D: quoted in Englander, Norman, O'Day and Owens: op. cit., pp. 346–8.

Source E: *The Tribute Money* (Titian); *The Holy Trinity* (El Greco).

Source F: quoted in James Casey: *Early Modern Spain: A Social History* (London 1999), p. 68.

Source G: quoted in James Casey: ibid., p. 95.

Source H: derived from figures in J. Vicens Vives: *Economic History of Spain* (Barcelona 1959) and in J. H. Elliott: *Imperial Spain 1469–1716* (London 1981).

SELECT BIBLIOGRAPHY

All the general text books on early modern Europe have chapters on this period of the history of Spain. Among the most readable and accessible are: G. R. Elton: *Reformation Europe 1517–1559* (London 1963); and John Lotherington (ed.): *Years of Renewal: European History 1470–1600* (London 1988). Overviews of how the history of Spain, and particularly the overseas empire, affected Europe as a whole, can be found in Carlo M. Cipolla: *European Culture and Overseas Expansion* (London 1970) and the long but readable classic by Fernand Braudel: *The Mediterranean and the Mediterranean World in the Age of Philip II* (London 1971–3), 2 volumes.

Books on Spain during the sixteenth century include: Henry Kamen: *Spain 1469–1716: A Society in Conflict* (London 1983); and John Lynch: *Spain Under the Habsburgs*, Vol. 1: *Empire and Absolutism 1516–1598* (Oxford 1964). J. H. Elliott: *Imperial Spain: 1469–1716* (London 1963) is particularly clear about the financial and economic implications of the American silver. Other useful books about the Spanish empire in America are J. H. Parry: *The Age of Reconnaissance* (London 1963) and *The Spanish Seaborne Empire* (London 1973). A detailed account of society in Spain can be found in James Casey: *Early Modern Spain, A Social History* (London 1999).

FERDINAND AND ISABELLA

The most recent and thorough coverage of the reign of the Catholic monarchs can be found in Geoffrey Woodward: *Spain in the Reigns of Ferdinand and Isabella* (London 1997). A detailed study of their administrative methods is Marvin Lunenfeld: *Keepers of the City. The Corregidors of Isabella I of Castile 1474–1504* (Cambridge 1987). The background to their policies in Granada is explained in D. W. Lomax: *The Reconquest of Spain* (London 1978).

CHARLES I

Very readable and accessible are Martin Rady: *The Emperor Charles V* (London 1988) and Stewart Macdonald: *Charles V* (London 1992). For more detail on Charles himself, and particularly illustrations of him and his family, the classic is Karl Brandi: *The Emperor Charles V* (London 1939). Specifically on Spain, I. A. A. Thompson: *Crown and Cortes* (Aldershot 1993) and Stephen Haliczer: *The Communeros of Castile: The Forging of a Revolution 1475–1521* (Wisconsin 1981) can be recommended.

PHILIP II

Geoffrey Woodward: *Philip II* (London 1992) is the only summary available, but many historians have written very interestingly on Philip. A biography with plenty of controversial conclusions is Henry Kamen: *Philip of Spain* (New Haven CT and London 1997). A book which is difficult to put down as well as very useful is Geoffrey Parker: *The Grand Strategy of Philip II* (New Haven CT and London 1998).

Although Philip probably wrote more in his own hand than any other king in history, the only way to read his thought processes is through the historians (like Henry Kamen and Geoffrey Parker) who have used his words in their work. On the other hand, it is much easier to obtain anti-Philip propaganda, since it is available in English! One example is the *Explanation of the True and Lawful Right and title of the most Excellent Prince Anthonie* (Leyden, Christopher Plantyn's Printing House 1585; published under licence from Maurice, Earl of Nassau).

Collections of primary sources in English specifically on Spain in this period are not plentiful, although *Documents and Debates: Sixteenth Century Europe* (London 1984), edited by Katherine Leach, contains some. It is easier to find documents about

English attitudes to Spain, for example in: *Calendar of Letters, Despatches and State Papers relating to the negotiations between England and Spain*, Vol. 1: *1485–1509*, ed. G. A. Bergenroth (London 1862); *Letters and Papers of the Reign of Henry VIII*, ed. J. S. Brewer (London 1867); *English Historical Documents 1485–1558*, ed. C. H. Williams (London 1967).

INDEX

9402337R00090

Printed in Great Britain
by Amazon.co.uk, Ltd.,
Marston Gate.